CW01647609

بسم الله الرحمن الرحيم

Be Mindful of Allah

Be Mindful of Allah

Nūr al-Iqtibās fī

Mishkāt Waṣiyyat an-Nabī ﷺ li-Ibn ʿAbbās

IBN RAJAB AL-ḤANBALĪ

(736–795/1336–1393)

TURATH PUBLISHING

Copyright: Turath Publishing 1443/2022
ISBN: 978-1-906949-95-2

Published by:
Turath Publishing
84 Mitcham Road London SW17 9NG
www.turath.co.uk +44 (20) 8767 8613

All rights reserved. No part of this publication may be reproduced, stored in any retrieval system, or transmitted in any form or by any means, electronic or otherwise, without written permission of the publishers.

Author Ibn Rajab al-Ḥanbalī
Translator Shoaib Shah
Editor Andrew Booso
General Editors Yahya & Safira Batha

British Library Cataloguing in Publication Data
Nūr al-Iqtibās fī Mishkāt Waṣiyyat an-Nabī ﷺ li-Ibn ʿAbbās

Design & Typesetting ARM (www.whitethreadpress.com)
Printed by Mega Print, Istanbul

Distributors for UK and Europe
Azhar Academy Ltd.
54–56 Little Ilford Lane, London E12 5QA
trade@azharacademy.com
www.azharacademy.com

Distributors for South Africa
Darul-Ihsan Research and Education Centre
www.darulihsan.com

فمرحبًا بِعِبَادِي الَّذِينَ حَفِظُوا وَصِيَّتِي وَرَعَوْا عَهْدِي
وَخَافُونِي بِالْغَيْبِ وَكَانُوا مِنِّي عَلَى كُلِّ حَالٍ مُشْفِقِينَ

Greetings to My slaves! Those who are mindful of
My counsel, who observe My covenant, who fear Me,
though I am Unseen, and who love Me in any situation.

Contents

Translator's Foreword

All praise is for Allah, Lord of all the worlds; and may the peace and blessings of Allah be upon His chosen Prophet, Muhammad, his family and all of his Companions.

Allah ﷻ says,

﴿وَأَوْفُوا بِعَهْدِي أُوفِ بِعَهْدِكُمْ وَإِيَّايَ فَارْهَبُونِ﴾

Honour My contract and I will honour your contract, and fear only Me. (2:40)

And He ﷻ says,

﴿إِنِّي مَعَكُمْ لَئِنْ أَقَمْتُمُ الصَّلَاةَ وَآتَيْتُمُ الزَّكَاةَ وَآمَنْتُمْ بِرُسُلِي وَعَزَّرْتُمُوهُمْ وَأَقْرَضْتُمُ اللَّهَ قَرْضًا حَسَنًا لَأُكَفِّرَنَّ عَنْكُمْ سَيِّئَاتِكُمْ وَلَأُدْخِلَنَّكُمْ جَنَّاتٍ تَجْرِي مِنْ تَحْتِهَا الْأَنْهَارُ فَمَنْ كَفَرَ بَعْدَ ذَٰلِكَ مِنْكُمْ فَقَدْ ضَلَّ سَوَاءَ السَّبِيلِ﴾

I am with you. If you establish the prayer and pay zakat, and believe in My messengers and respect and support them, and make a generous loan to Allah, I will erase your wrong actions from you and admit you into Gardens with rivers flowing under them. Any of you who disbelieve after that have gone astray from the right way. (5:12)

Through heavenly revelation, Allah ﷻ blessed the Prophet ﷺ with the knowledge of Islam and the truth of our purpose in life. He ﷻ also promised the Prophet ﷺ that His Religion would prevail and spread to all corners of the world. People of the world would, someday, look to Islam for answers, so the Prophet ﷺ, anticipating this need, entrusted his faithful Companions ﷺ with the necessary tools to navigate through this perilous life and arrive safely at Allah ﷻ in the Hereafter. Every word he spoke was a direction, every move he made a map and every approval he gave a signpost. He then encouraged his Companions ﷺ, 'Convey these messages from me; even if it be a single verse.'[1] The Companions ﷺ obediently passed on these precious instructions, in hopes that later generations could learn our true purpose and also appreciate but a glimmer of the Prophet's ﷺ light.

Thereafter came the scholars of Hadith, who truly exceeded all expectations in their collections of these maps and manuals and their critical analysis thereof, distinguishing the legitimate content from the fraudulent and doubtful. Today, we have these manuals in our hands, and Allah has blessed this nation further with exemplary scholars who dedicated their lives to understanding them, pondering over them and unlocking the treasures hidden within. The famed eighth-century traditionist, Ibn Rajab al-Ḥanbalī and his meticulous in-depth study of a hadith of Ibn ʿAbbās ﷺ is a perfect example of this; a truly comprehensive and expansive look at one of the many advices the Prophet ﷺ gave to his Companions.

This hadith is a brief but comprehensive look at the rights we owe Allah ﷻ and His guarantees if we fulfil those rights; and, to this end, it stresses the importance of having *taqwā*. *Taqwā* is not restricted to fear of Allah ﷻ; rather, it is being conscious of Allah ﷻ and mindful of our responsibilities as His slaves.

ʿUmar ibn al-Khaṭṭāb ﷺ once asked Ubayy ibn Kaʿb ﷺ, 'What is *taqwā*?' Ubayy responded, 'Commander of the Believers, have you ever walked a path surrounded by thorny bushes? ʿUmar said, 'Yes.' 'What did you do on that path,' asked Ubayy. ʿUmar said, 'I gathered my clothes, holding them close to me and tried to stay away from the thorns as much as possible.' Ubayy said, 'That is *taqwā*.'[2]

1 Bukhārī (3461).

2 Ibn Kathīr, 1:164.

The hadith also discusses the fundamental beliefs of Allah's oneness (*tawḥīd*) and destiny, and it ends with advice on tackling life with patience and unyielding supplication when matters are testing. In this commentary, Ibn Rajab takes us on a thought-provoking journey through the hadith of Ibn ʿAbbās ﷺ, as quoted by Aḥmad, Tirmidhī and others.

Ibn Rajab has commented on this hadith with a brief overview in his book *The Compendium of Knowledge and Wisdom*, and he has specifically made reference to this detailed treatise. He begins the book by presenting the hadith and critically analysing its many variations and multiple chains of transmission, thereby establishing its place among the many reliable narrations from the Prophet ﷺ. Each point of advice the Prophet ﷺ gave Ibn ʿAbbās ﷺ is deconstructed and presented as the heading of a new chapter, which he dissects, explaining it in depth by corroborating it with verses and narrations that complement the advice. In his wonderful style, he searches the Qur'an and the numerous collections of hadith for similar content that discusses safeguarding or being mindful (*ḥifẓ*) in all its various forms, thereby adding multiple layers to a single statement. He also supplements the statements with verses and narrations that do not mention the word *ḥifẓ* but discuss the same basic meaning. In doing so, he presents a full and complete picture of what the Religion of Islam requires of us, with all the available material on the subject, not a single statement, quoted out of context and, subsequently, misconstrued and misunderstood.

He supplements all of the verses and hadiths with insightful incidents and real life experiences from early Muslim generations that confirm and establish what Allah ﷻ has mentioned and the Prophet ﷺ conveyed. He also includes short but powerful poems from the early pious Muslims to soften our hearts.

Although the title of the original Arabic book is *Nūr al-Iqtibās fī Mishkāt Waṣiyyat an-Nabī ﷺ li-Ibn ʿAbbās,* we have chosen the first advice of the hadith, 'Be mindful of Allah,' as the title of the English translation, because it succinctly encapsulates *taqwā*, a core tenet of

Islam. We have added references for the hadiths and a bibliography for the works cited by Ibn Rajab. We have also added sub-headings, not found in the original, to make the discussion more coherent and easier to follow.

We pray that Allah ﷻ facilitates this book as a means to bring us closer to Him and allow His love and the love of His beloved Prophet ﷺ to pierce our hard hearts and occupy them eternally. May Allah ﷻ reward the author with mercy and relief on the Day of Rising and endless blessings in the highest levels of Paradise. May He ﷻ also extend His mercy and blessings to the publisher, the translator, all those who assisted in this publication and the whole of the nation of our beloved Prophet Muhammad ﷺ. *Āmīn*

Shoaib Shah
Leicester
Turath Publishing

Author's Introduction

In the name of Allah, All-Merciful, Most Merciful.

All praise is for Allah, pure, blessed and plentiful praise, as our Lord loves and is pleased with and as is befitting to His Honourable Countenance ﷻ. And may the blessings and innumerable peace of Allah ﷻ be upon Muhammad, the unlettered Prophet, his family and his Companions.

Imam Aḥmad quotes from the hadith of Ḥanash aṣ-Ṣanʿānī who relates that Ibn ʿAbbās ﵄ said,

كُنْتُ رَدِيفَ رَسُولِ اللهِ ﷺ، فَقَالَ: يَا غُلَامُ – أَوْ يَا غُلَيِّمُ – أَلَا أُعَلِّمُكَ كَلِمَاتٍ يَنْفَعُكَ اللهُ بِهِنَّ؟ فَقُلْتُ: بَلَى. فَقَالَ: احْفَظِ اللهَ يَحْفَظْكَ، احْفَظِ اللهَ تَجِدْهُ أَمَامَكَ، تَعَرَّفْ إِلَيْهِ فِي الرَّخَاءِ، يَعْرِفْكَ فِي الشِّدَّةِ، وَإِذَا سَأَلْتَ، فَاسْأَلِ اللهَ، وَإِذَا اسْتَعَنْتَ، فَاسْتَعِنْ بِاللهِ قَدْ جَفَّ الْقَلَمُ بِمَا هُوَ كَائِنٌ، فَلَوْ أَنَّ الْخَلْقَ كُلَّهُمْ جَمِيعًا أَرَادُوا أَنْ يَنْفَعُوكَ بِشَيْءٍ لَمْ يَكْتُبْهُ اللهُ عَلَيْكَ، لَمْ يَقْدِرُوا عَلَيْهِ، وَإِنْ أَرَادُوا أَنْ يَضُرُّوكَ بِشَيْءٍ لَمْ يَكْتُبْهُ اللهُ عَلَيْكَ، لَمْ يَقْدِرُوا عَلَيْهِ، وَاعْلَمْ أَنَّ فِي الصَّبْرِ عَلَى مَا تَكْرَهُ خَيْرًا كَثِيرًا، وَأَنَّ النَّصْرَ مَعَ الصَّبْرِ، وَأَنَّ الْفَرَجَ مَعَ الْكَرْبِ، وَأَنَّ مَعَ الْعُسْرِ يُسْرًا.

I was riding behind the Prophet ﷺ when he said, 'O child (or O little child)! Shall I not teach you some words through which Allah will benefit you?' I answered, 'Of course.' He ﷺ said, 'Be

> mindful of Allah and He will be mindful of you. Be mindful of Allah and you will find Him in front of you. Become acquainted with Allah in times of ease and He will recognise you in times of hardship. When you ask, ask Allah; and when you seek assistance, seek it from Allah. The pens have dried regarding what is to be; if all of creation together wanted to benefit you with something that Allah has not destined, they would not be able to do it. And if they wanted to harm you with something that Allah has not ordained against you, they would not be able to do it. Know that much good comes from patience in the face of adversity. Know that victory comes with patience, relief comes with grief and that with hardship comes ease.'[1]

This is the variation related from Ḥanash, with two other incomplete chains. Imam Aḥmad also mentions that he does not remember one from the other. He has, however, quoted it in an abridged form only from Ḥanash with the following words:

> O child! I am going to tell you something: Be mindful of Allah and He will be mindful of you. Be mindful of Allah and you will find Him facing you. When you ask, ask Allah; and when you seek assistance, seek it from Allah. The pens have been lifted and the pages have dried. If the whole nation came to benefit you with something which Allah has not ordained for you, they would not be able to. And if they wanted to harm you with something which Allah has not ordained for you, they would not be able to.[2]

Tirmidhī has quoted a similar abridged version in the following words:

> I will teach you some words: Be mindful of Allah and He will be mindful of you. Be mindful of Allah and you will find Him facing you. When you ask, ask Allah; and when you seek assistance, seek it from Allah. Know that if the whole nation came together to benefit you with something, they would not be able to benefit you with anything

1 Aḥmad (2803).
2 Aḥmad (2763).

> except what Allah has ordained for you. And if they came together to harm you with something, they would not be able to harm you with anything except what Allah has ordained against you. The pens have been lifted and the pages have dried.[1]

Tirmidhī said this is a sound (*ḥasan*), authentic (*ṣaḥīḥ*) hadith.

Ḥāfiẓ Abū Abdillāh ibn Mandah said, 'This hadith has many chains of transmission from Ibn ʿAbbās ﷺ, the most authentic of which is this.' He goes on to say, 'This is a well-known chain and its narrators are reliable.'

This hadith of Ibn ʿAbbās ﷺ has been related from many narrators with many variations; additions and omissions in the wording of the hadith. Some of them are his son ʿAlī, ʿAṭā' and ʿIkrimah. It has also been related from ʿUmar, the freed slave of Ghafrah, who relates from Ibn ʿAbbās ﷺ. ʿAbd al-Malik ibn ʿUmayr and Ibn Abī Mulaykah also relate from Ibn ʿAbbās ﷺ, however some scholars say the latter two did not hear from him directly. There is also some discussion about them in the chains of transmission.

It has also been related directly from the Prophet ﷺ that he advised Ibn ʿAbbās ﷺ of the same [advice] from other Companions ﷺ, such as ʿAlī ibn Abī Ṭālib, Abū Saʿīd al-Khudrī, Sahl ibn Saʿd and others ﷺ. Scholars have also discussed much about he chains of transmission for these variations too. ʿUqaylī mentions that all of the chains of the hadith are compromised, although some are more authentic than others. The most authentic chain, however, is Ḥanash's, who relates from Ibn ʿAbbās ﷺ, as we have mentioned; it is a sound chain which has no problems. We have exhausted the list of the chains of this hadith with a discussion in the book *Sharḥ at-Tirmidhī*.

Our purpose in this book is to discuss the meaning of the hadith and to expound on its words, since they contain great counsel and comprehensive principles from the most important and most significant aspects of the religion. Accordingly, Imam Abū 'l-Faraj [Ibn al-Jawzī] said in his book *Ṣayd al-Khāṭir*, 'I pondered on this hadith

1 Tirmidhī (2516).

and it amazed me until I was almost perplexed.' He then said, 'Oh how unfortunate is the ignorance towards this hadith and the lack of understanding in its meanings!'

CHAPTER 1

Be Mindful of Allah ﷻ

This means: be mindful of the limits of Allah ﷻ, His rights, His commands and His prohibitions. Being mindful of His commands is to carry them out and being mindful of His prohibitions is to refrain from them. Mindfulness of His limits is to not transgress from what He has commanded, thereby falling into what He has prohibited. Hence, this includes fulfilling all obligations and leaving all that is forbidden, as is mentioned in the hadith of Abū Thaʿlabah ﷺ from the Prophet ﷺ:

إِنَّ اللهَ ﷻ فَرَضَ فَرَائِضَ فَلَا تُضَيِّعُوهَا، وَحَرَّمَ حُرُمَاتٍ فَلَا تَنْتَهِكُوهَا، وَحَدَّ حُدُودًا فَلَا تَعْتَدُوهَا.

> Allah ﷻ has prescribed obligations; do not neglect them! He has delineated prohibitions; do not abuse them! He has fixed boundaries; do not transgress them![1]

All of the aforementioned is encompassed in being mindful of the limits of Allah ﷻ, as He says,

﴿وَالْحَافِظُونَ لِحُدُودِ اللهِ وَبَشِّرِ الْمُؤْمِنِينَ﴾

Those who preserve the limits of Allah (9:112).

---

1 Dāraquṭnī (4396).

Allah ﷻ also says,

﴿هَذَا مَا تُوعَدُونَ لِكُلِّ أَوَّابٍ حَفِيظٍ ﴿٣٢﴾ مَنْ خَشِيَ الرَّحْمَنَ بِالْغَيْبِ وَجَاءَ بِقَلْبٍ مُنِيبٍ ﴿٣٣﴾﴾

This is what you were promised. It is for every careful (ḥafīẓ) penitent: those who fear the All-Merciful in the Unseen and come with a contrite heart. (50:32–33)

The word *ḥafīẓ* here means the one who fulfils the commands of Allah ﷻ and is mindful of his sins, always returning to Allah [if he lapses]. Another possible meaning of *ḥafīẓ* is the one who is mindful of Allah's counsel to His slaves and carries them. All of these have the same basic meaning.

It has been mentioned in some variations of the hadith about the Day of Abundance in Paradise, that Allah ﷻ will say to the people of Paradise, when He ﷻ invites them to visit Him and the veils are lifted from them,

فَمَرْحَبًا بِعِبَادِي الَّذِينَ حَفِظُوا وَصِيَّتِي وَرَعَوْا عَهْدِي وَخَافُونِي بِالْغَيْبِ، وَكَانُوا مِنِّي عَلَى كُلِّ حَالٍ مُشْفِقِينَ.

Greetings to My slaves! Those who are mindful of My counsel, who observe My covenant, who fear Me, though I am Unseen, and who love Me in any situation.[1]

Therefore, the Prophet's ﷺ command to Ibn ʿAbbās ﷺ to be mindful of Allah ﷻ includes all of the above.

[BE MINDFUL OF THE PRAYER]

The most significant obligation that must be guarded is the five daily prayers. Allah ﷻ says,

1 Ibn Abī 'd-Dunyā, *Ṣifat al-Jannah* (51).

﴿حَافِظُوا عَلَى الصَّلَوَاتِ وَالصَّلَاةِ الْوُسْطَى﴾

Safeguard the prayer—especially the middle one. (2:238)

Allah ﷻ also says,

﴿وَالَّذِينَ هُمْ عَلَى صَلَاتِهِمْ يُحَافِظُونَ﴾

And those who safeguard their prayer. (70:34)

The Prophet ﷺ said,

مَنْ حَافَظَ عَلَيْهَا. . كَانَ لَهُ عِنْدَ اللهِ عَهْدٌ أَنْ يُدْخِلَهُ الْجَنَّةَ.

Whoever guards them [. . .] will have a covenant with Allah that He will enter him in to Paradise.[1]

It is mentioned in another hadith,

مَنْ حَافَظَ عَلَيْهِنَّ، كُنَّ لَهُ نُورًا وَبُرْهَانًا وَنَجَاةً يَوْمَ الْقِيَامَةِ.

'Whoever guards them will have light, a clear proof and salvation on the Day of Rising.'[2] Likewise, cleanliness [must also be guarded], as it is the key to prayer. The Prophet ﷺ said,

لَا يُحَافِظُ عَلَى الْوُضُوءِ إِلَّا مُؤْمِنٌ.

Only a true believer would be mindful of the ablution.[3]

This is evident because, when the slave's ablution is invalidated, no one but Allah ﷻ knows [if he was to pray without renewing his *wuḍū*]. Therefore, being mindful of the ablution for prayer is a proof of the strength of belief in one's heart.

[BE MINDFUL OF OATHS]

Oaths are another example of what Allah ﷻ has commanded to be safeguarded, as He ﷻ says regarding the expiation of oaths:

---

1 Mālik quotes a variation of this hadith (400).

2 Ṭabarāni, *Awsaṭ* (1767).

3 Ibn Ḥibbān (1037)

﴿ذَٰلِكَ كَفَّارَةُ أَيْمَانِكُمْ إِذَا حَلَفْتُمْ وَاحْفَظُوا أَيْمَانَكُمْ﴾

That is the expiation of breaking oaths when you have sworn them. Keep your oaths. (5:89)

People tend to frequently make vows, and their consequences vary. Sometimes offering expiation for the oath becomes necessary, other times offering a binding expiation is necessary, and sometimes divorce and other such things become legally binding upon the one against whom the oath was made. So, safeguarding of one's oaths is an indication that belief has entered the heart.

The early Muslims were very meticulous in safeguarding their oaths. Some of them would never swear by Allah ﷻ at all, while others were so God-fearing that they would make an act of expiation if they were doubtful about [fulfilling] a vow they made. Imam Aḥmad made a bequest on his deathbed for a payment to be made on his behalf as expiation of an oath, reasoning, 'I think I broke an oath that I took.'

It is related about Ayyūb عليه السلام that if he passed by two people swearing by Allah ﷻ, he would give expiation on behalf of both their oaths, so that they would not fall into sin unknowingly. For this reason, when he vowed to strike his wife 100 times, Allah ﷻ gave him a verdict of concession, since he would safeguard his own oaths and the oaths of others. Scholars differ on whether the concession extends to others or not.

Yazīd ibn Abī Ḥabīb said,

> It has reached me that one of the angels who carry the Throne cries rivers of tears. When he lifts his head, he says, 'Pure You are! You are not feared as You should be feared!' Then Allah ﷻ will say, 'But those who fallaciously swear by My name do not know that.'

One faces great severity by taking fallacious oaths, since swearing excessive oaths by Allah ﷻ is a product of one's ignorance of Allah and the lack of awe of Him in one's heart.

[BE MINDFUL OF THE HEAD AND STOMACH]

The head and stomach are further examples of what a believer should safeguard, as can be seen from the hadith of Ibn Masʿūd ﵁ from the Prophet ﷺ, as quoted by Imam Aḥmad and Tirmidhī,

الِاسْتِحْيَاءَ مِنَ اللهِ. حَقَّ الحَيَاءِ أَنْ تَحْفَظَ الرَّأْسَ وَمَا وَعَى، وَالبَطْنَ وَمَا حَوَى.

> Modesty demands shame before Allah ﷻ. An individual should guard his head and what it retains and guard his internal body and what it contains.[1]

Guarding the head and what it retains includes protecting the hearing, sight and tongue from prohibitions. Guarding one's internal body and its contents includes protecting the heart from persistent sinning. Allah ﷻ has encompassed all of these in His words:

﴿إِنَّ السَّمْعَ وَالْبَصَرَ وَالْفُؤَادَ كُلُّ أُولَٰئِكَ كَانَ عَنْهُ مَسْئُولًا﴾

> *Hearing, sight and hearts will all be questioned.* (17:36)

Another aspect of guarding the internal body and its contents is to protect it from the ingestion of unlawful food and drink.

[BE MINDFUL OF THE TONGUE AND PRIVATE PARTS]

The tongue and the private parts are two more examples of things that must be guarded from prohibitions, as is is mentioned in the hadith of Abū Hurayrah ﵁ from the Prophet ﷺ, quoted by Ḥākim,

مَنْ حَفِظَ مَا بَيْنَ لَحْيَيْهِ وَ مَا بَيْنَ رِجْلَيْهِ دَخَلَ الجَنَّةَ.

> 'Whoever guards what is between his jaws and what is between his legs will enter Paradise.'[2] Bukhārī relates a variation from the hadith of Sahl ibn Saʿd ﵁ from the Prophet ﷺ:

---

1 Aḥmad (3671); Tirmidhī (2458).

2 Ḥākim (8058).

مَنْ يَضْمَنْ لِي مَا بَيْنَ لَحْيَيْهِ وَمَا بَيْنَ رِجْلَيْهِ أَضْمَنْ لَهُ الجَنَّةَ.

> If an individual secures what is between his jaws and his legs, I will secure Paradise for him.[1]

Another variation is quoted in the *Musnad* of Imam Aḥmad from Abū Mūsā ﷺ that the Prophet ﷺ said,

مَنْ حَفِظَ مَا بَيْنَ فُقْمَيْهِ وَفَرْجَهُ دَخَلَ الْجَنَّةَ.

> Whoever guards what is between his jaws and his private parts will enter Paradise.[2]

Allah ﷻ has commanded the guarding of the private parts specifically in the Qur'an, commending those who do so:

﴿قُلْ لِلْمُؤْمِنِينَ يَغُضُّوا مِنْ أَبْصَارِهِمْ وَيَحْفَظُوا فُرُوجَهُم﴾

> *Say to the believers that they should lower their eyes and guard their private parts.* (24:30)

He ﷻ also says,

﴿وَالْحَافِظِينَ فُرُوجَهُمْ وَالْحَافِظَاتِ. . .أَعَدَّ اللهُ لَهُمْ مَغْفِرَةً وَأَجْرًا عَظِيمًا﴾

> *Men and women who guard their private parts* [. . .] *Allah has prepared forgiveness for them and an immense reward.* (33:35)

Allah ﷻ also says,

﴿وَالَّذِينَ هُمْ لِفُرُوجِهِمْ حَافِظُونَ ۝ إِلَّا عَلَى أَزْوَاجِهِمْ أَوْ مَا مَلَكَتْ أَيْمَانُهُمْ فَإِنَّهُمْ غَيْرُ مَلُومِينَ ۝﴾

> *Those who guard their private parts—except from their wives or those they own as slaves, in which case they are not blameworthy.* (23:5–6)

Abū Idrīs al-Khawlānī said, 'The first instruction Allah ﷻ gave to Ādam ﷺ when he sent him down to earth was to guard his private parts and to not use it except in a lawful way.'

1 Bukhārī (6474).
2 Aḥmad (19559).

CHAPTER 2

He ﷻ Will Be Mindful of You

This means: whoever guards the limits of Allah ﷻ and takes care of His rights, Allah ﷻ will safeguard him. A reward will [often] resemble the deed, as Allah ﷻ says,

﴿وَأَوْفُوا بِعَهْدِى أُوفِ بِعَهْدِكُمْ﴾

Honour My contract and I will honour your contract. (2:40)

﴿فَاذْكُرُونِى أَذْكُرْكُمْ﴾

Remember Me, I will remember you. (2:152)

﴿إِنْ تَنْصُرُوا اللَّهَ يَنْصُرْكُمْ﴾

If you help Allah, He will help you. (47:7)

[HE ﷻ WILL PROTECT YOUR WORLDLY INTERESTS]

There are two ways in which Allah ﷻ safeguards His slaves. Firstly, He safeguards their worldly interests; their bodies, their children, their families and their wealth. Regarding this, Imam Aḥmad, Abū Dāwūd, Nasā'ī and Ibn Mājah report that Ibn ʿUmar ﷺ said,

> The Messenger of Allah ﷺ would, without fail, recite the following supplications in the evening and the morning:

اللَّهُمَّ إِنِّي أَسْأَلُكَ الْعَافِيَةَ فِي الدُّنْيَا وَالْآخِرَةِ، اللَّهُمَّ إِنِّي أَسْأَلُكَ الْعَفْوَ وَالْعَافِيَةَ فِي دِينِي وَدُنْيَايَ وَأَهْلِي وَمَالِي، اللَّهُمَّ اسْتُرْ عَوْرَاتِي، وَآمِنْ رَوْعَاتِي، اللَّهُمَّ احْفَظْنِي مِنْ بَيْنِ يَدَيَّ، وَمِنْ خَلْفِي، وَعَنْ يَمِينِي، وَعَنْ شِمَالِي، وَمِنْ فَوْقِي، وَأَعُوذُ بِعَظَمَتِكَ أَنْ أُغْتَالَ مِنْ تَحْتِي.

> O Allah! I ask You for well-being in this life and the Hereafter. O Allah! I ask You for pardon and well-being in my life, my religion, my family and my wealth. O Allah! Conceal my imperfections and secure my awe. Guard me from in front of me, from behind me, from my right and my left, and from above me. I seek refuge, in Your Greatness, from being deceived from beneath me.[1]

This supplication has been extracted from the words of Allah ﷻ:

﴿لَهُ مُعَقِّبَاتٌ مِنْ بَيْنِ يَدَيْهِ وَمِنْ خَلْفِهِ يَحْفَظُونَهُ مِنْ أَمْرِ اللَّهِ﴾

> *Everyone has a succession of angels in front of him and behind him, guarding him by Allah's command.* (13:11)

Ibn ʿAbbās ﷺ explained the verse, saying, 'They are the angels who guard him by the command of Allah ﷻ. And when fate strikes, they leave him.'

ʿAlī ﷺ said, 'Every man has two angels who guard him from what is not destined for him. If, however, fate strikes, they leave him be. Indeed, [the fate of] death is fortified and strong.'

Mujāhid said,

> Every slave of Allah ﷻ has an angel who guards him from jinn, humans and madness, in his sleep and when he is awake. If anything approaches him, they say to it, 'Turn back,' except for those things Allah ﷻ has allowed, which will inevitably afflict him.

---

1 Aḥmad (4785); Abū Dāwūd (5074); Nasāʾī, *as-Sunan al-Kubrā* (10325); Ibn Mājah (3871).

[HE ﷻ WILL PROTECT YOUR BODY]

An example of how Allah ﷻ safeguards His slaves is the preservation of their bodies, their strength, their intellect and their wealth.. One of the early Muslims said, (in this respect,) 'A scholar does not become senile.' Others have interpreted from the words of Allah ﷻ that the memoriser of the Qur'an will benefit much from his intellect:

﴿ثُمَّ رَدَدْنَاهُ أَسْفَلَ سَافِلِينَ ۝٥ إِلَّا الَّذِينَ آمَنُوا وَعَمِلُوا الصَّالِحَاتِ ۝٦﴾

Then We reduced him to the lowest of the low, except for those who believe and do right actions. (95:5–6)

Abū 'ṭ-Ṭīb aṭ-Ṭabarī lived over 100 years, benefitting from his intellect and his strength. On one occasion, he leapt ashore, vigorously jumping from a boat, and was subsequently reproached for it. He explained, 'We guarded these limbs from sins in [our] youth, so Allah ﷻ has maintained them for us in old age.' The opposite is also true, as is demonstrated when Junayd saw a man asking from people. He noted, 'This man neglected Allah ﷻ in youth, so Allah neglected him in old age.'

[HE ﷻ WILL PROTECT YOUR CHILDREN]

Sometimes Allah ﷻ also safeguards His slave's children, and their children, because of his own piety. He ﷻ says that He protected [and kept hidden the treasure belonging to two orphans] because of their father's piety:

﴿كَانَ أَبُوهُمَا صَالِحًا﴾

Their father was one of the righteous. (18:82)[1]

Muhammad ibn al-Munkadir said, 'Because of a pious man, Allah ﷻ safeguards his children and their children, the city where he lives and

1 See 18:77 and 82.

the dwellings surrounding it. They constantly remain in the protection and shelter of Allah ﷻ.'

Ibn al-Musayyab once said, 'My son! I increase my prayers for your sake, hoping that it will protect you,' then justifying it by reciting: *Their father was one of the righteous* [18:82].

Additionally, ʿUmar ibn ʿAbd al-ʿAzīz said, 'No believer dies but Allah ﷻ safeguards his progeny and their progeny.'

Yaḥyā ibn Ismāʿīl ibn Salamah ibn Kuhayl said,

> I had an elder sister who kept herself in isolation because she went mad, rambling deliriously. She had a room at the furthest end of our terrace where she stayed for ten or twenty years. One night, while I was sleeping in the middle of the night, someone knocked on the door. I asked, 'Who is it?' She said, 'Kajah.' I said, 'My sister?' She responded, 'Your sister.' So I opened the door and she entered, not having contact with the house for more than twenty years. She said, 'Someone came to me in my dream tonight and said, "Allah ﷻ has safeguarded your father Ismāʿīl for the sake of your grandfather Salamah and has safeguarded you for the sake of your father Ismāʿīl. If you wish, you may supplicate to Allah to remove your affliction; or if you wish, you may persevere and you will have Paradise. Abū Bakr and ʿUmar interceded on your behalf to Allah ﷻ because of your father's and grandfather's love for them." I said, "If I am to choose one, I choose to persevere in my affliction to attain Paradise. However, Allah is extremely generous to His creation and nothing is too great for him. If He wills, He can bestow them both upon me." Then I was told, "Allah ﷻ has bestowed them both upon you and He is pleased with your father and grandfather for their love of Abū Bakr and ʿUmar. Stand and proceed."' Then Allah removed her affliction.

When a slave of Allah ﷻ constantly obeys Him, Allah ﷻ will, in turn, safeguard him, as is mentioned in the *Musnad* of Imam Aḥmad related from Ḥumayd ibn Hilāl who says that a Companion said,

فَانْتَهَيْتُ إِلَى رَسُولِ اللهِ ﷺ، فَإِذَا هُوَ يُرِينِي بَيْتًا، قَالَ: إِنَّ امْرَأَةً كَانَتْ فِيهِ فَخَرَجَتْ فِي سَرِيَّةٍ مِنَ الْمُسْلِمِينَ، وَتَرَكَتْ ثِنْتَيْ عَشْرَةَ عَنْزًا لَهَا وَصِيصِيَتَهَا كَانَتْ تَنْسِجُ بِهَا. قَالَ: فَفَقَدَتْ عَنْزًا مِنْ غَنَمِهَا وَصِيصِيَتَهَا، فَقَالَتْ: يَا رَبِّ، إِنَّكَ قَدْ ضَمِنْتَ لِمَنْ خَرَجَ فِي سَبِيلِكَ أَنْ تَحْفَظَ عَلَيْهِ، وَإِنِّي قَدْ فَقَدْتُ عَنْزًا مِنْ غَنَمِي وَصِيصِيَتِي، وَإِنِّي أَنْشُدُكَ عَنْزِي وَصِيصِيَتِي. قَالَ: فَجَعَلَ رَسُولُ اللهِ ﷺ يَذْكُرُ شِدَّةَ مُنَاشَدَتِهَا لِرَبِّهَا تَبَارَكَ وَتَعَالَى، قَالَ رَسُولُ اللهِ ﷺ: فَأَصْبَحَتْ عَنْزُهَا وَمِثْلُهَا، وَصِيصِيَتُهَا وَمِثْلُهَا، وَهَاتِيكَ فَأْتِهَا فَاسْأَلْهَا إِنْ شِئْتَ. قَالَ: قُلْتُ: بَلْ أُصَدِّقُكَ.

I came to the Prophet ﷺ; when I got there, he began showing me a house and saying, 'There is a woman who lives here, who decided to go (in the path of Allah) with a detachment of Muslims, leaving twelve goats and a hook for weaving behind. She then lost a goat and her hook, so she said, "My Lord! I have lost a goat from my herd and my hook, and You have promised to be responsible for anyone who goes out in Your path. I implore you regarding my goat and my hook,'" and the Messenger of Allah ﷺ mentioned how she earnestly implored her Lord ﷻ. The Messenger of Allah ﷺ said, 'The next morning, her goat and another just like it and her hook and another just like it appeared. Look! Go to her and ask her if you like.' I said, 'I believe you.'[1]

Another example is Shaybān the shepherd, who would graze his sheep in the desert, and every Friday, he would mark them with a line and make his way to the Friday prayer. On his return, he would find them as he left them. There was also one of the early Muslims, who would carry a scale in his hand to weigh dirhams. When he heard the call to prayer, he would leave for the prayer and cast them in the dust. When he returned nothing would be missing from it.

---

1 Aḥmad (20664).

[HE ﷻ WILL PROTECT YOU FROM MALICIOUS FORCES]

Another way that Allah ﷻ safeguards those who are mindful of Him and His Religion is that He protects them from the evil of any jinn or human who wishes to harm him. Allah ﷻ says,

﴿وَمَنْ يَتَّقِ اللَّهَ يَجْعَلْ لَهُ مَخْرَجًا﴾

Whoever fears Allah, He will give him a way out. (65:2)

ʿĀʾishah ﷺ explained [the verse], 'Allah ﷻ suffices him against the troubles and worries of the world.'

Rabīʿ ibn Khuthaym said, [offering another explanation,] 'He gives him a way out from all things that trouble people.'

ʿĀʾishah ﷺ once wrote to Muʿāwiyah ﷺ [about this]: 'If you fear Allah ﷻ, He will suffice you against people. But if you fear people, they will not avail you against Allah in the slightest.'

One of the Caliphs once wrote a letter to Ḥakam ibn ʿAmr al-Ghifārī, ordering him to take a course of action that contravened the Book of Allah, but Ḥakam wrote back:

> I looked at the Book of Allah ﷻ and I prefer it to the letter of the Leader of the Believers (*amīr al-muʾminīn*). If [all the troubles of] heavens and the earth were sewn together on a person['s garment], but he has fear of Allah ﷻ, He will surely give him a way out. Peace be with you.

One of the poets said,

> With the fear of Allah ﷻ, the successful achieved success
> They won the day and attained what they had hoped for
> Whoever fears Allah ﷻ, He will facilitate for him
> A way out of troubles, as He said in His command.

One of the early Muslims wrote to his brother, 'As to what follows: whoever fears Allah ﷻ has safeguarded himself; and whoever neglects Allah has neglected himself, and Allah is not in need of him.'

[HE ﷻ WILL PROTECT YOU THROUGH BEASTS]

An amazing way that Allah ﷻ safeguards those who are mindful of Him is that He transforms the nature of harmful animals, making them his protectors, assisting him in his interests. A similar incident took place with Safīnah ؓ, the Prophet's ﷺ freed slave, when his boat capsized. Washed ashore, he saw a lion, so he said, 'Lion! I am Safīnah, the freed slave of the Messenger of Allah ﷺ.' It then started walking around him, showing him the way until it took him to the main path. Then it growled, as though it was bidding him farewell, and left.

Abū Ibrāhīm as-Sā'iḥ once fell ill in a desert near a monastery and thought to himself, 'If only I was at the gate of the monastery, so that the monks could treat me.' Meanwhile, a lion came along and, lifting him onto its back, carried him until it dropped him at the gate of the monastery. When the monks saw this, they embraced Islam, all four hundred of them!

Once, Ibrāhīm ibn Adham was asleep in a garden and there was a snake near him with a bouquet of flowers in its mouth, fanning flies away from him until he awoke.

Hence, whoever is mindful of Allah ﷻ, Allah ﷻ will safeguard him from beasts and predators, commanding them to protect him instead. And whoever neglects Allah ﷻ, Allah ﷻ will neglect him through His creation, causing him harm from things he assumes will benefit him and people whose love and graciousness he expects. In this vein, one of the early Muslims said, 'When I disobey Allah ﷻ, I sense its effects in the bad attitude of my slave and my donkey.' What he means is that his slave's attitude becomes negative towards him and he does not obey him, and his donkey disobeys him and does not offer to carry him. Ultimately, all good is consolidated in the obedience of Allah ﷻ and drawing near to Him and all evil is consolidated in the disobedience of Allah ﷻ and turning away from Him.

One of the gnostics said, 'Whoever leaves the door of his Master will never find a stable-footing.'

A poet said,

By Allah, whenever I came to visit You
    I found the distance of the land shortened.
Whenever I turned my resolve away from Your door,
    I stumbled on my garment's hem.
So for Allah's sake, pardon, be kind and look past
    My shortcomings, for my state is the state you see.

[HE ﷻ WILL PROTECT YOUR RELIGION]

The second aspect to safeguarding, which it the best and the most excellent form of safeguarding—is Allah's ﷻ protection of His slave's religion. While he is alive, He safeguards his religion and belief from fatal doubts, misleading innovations and unlawful caprices. Thereafter, He ﷻ safeguards his religion at the crucial time of his death, taking his soul firm upon Islam. Ibn Abī 'd-Dunyā recorded that Ḥakam ibn Abān relates from Abū Makkī,

> When death approaches a man, the angel is told, 'Smell his head.' The angel will say, 'I can smell the Qur'an from his head.' Then he is told, 'Smell his heart.' He will say, 'I can smell fasts from his heart.' Then he will be told, 'Smell his feet.' He will say, 'I can smell the standing in prayer from his feet.' He will say, 'He protected himself, so Allah ﷻ has protected him.'

It is established in the *Ṣaḥīḥayn* from the hadith of Barā' ibn ʿĀzib ﷺ that the Prophet ﷺ taught him to say the following before sleeping:

إِنْ أَمْسَكْتَ نَفْسِي فَارْحَمْهَا، وَإِنْ أَرْسَلْتَهَا فَاحْفَظْهَا بِمَا تَحْفَظُ بِهِ عِبَادَكَ الصَّالِحِينَ.

> O Allah! If You seize my soul, have mercy on it; and if You release it, safeguard it the way You safeguard Your righteous slaves.[1]

Ibn Ḥibbān recorded in his *Ṣaḥīḥ* that the Prophet ﷺ taught ʿUmar ﷺ to say,

---

1 Bukhārī (6320); Muslim (2714). In both collections, Abū Hurayrah ﷺ is the narrator.

اللّٰهُمَّ احْفَظْنِي بِالْإِسْلَامِ قَاعِدًا، وَاحْفَظْنِي بِالْإِسْلَامِ قَائِمًا، وَاحْفَظْنِي بِالْإِسْلَامِ رَاقِدًا، وَلَا تُطِعْ فِيَّ عَدُوًّا حَاسِدًا.

O Allah! Keep me firm on Islam while standing, keep me firm on Islam while sitting, keep me firm on Islam while reclining and do not answer [the supplications of] any envious enemy to harm me.[1]

Whenever the Prophet ﷺ bid farewell to travellers, he would say,

أَسْتَوْدِعُ اللهَ دِينَكَ وَأَمَانَتَكَ وَخَوَاتِيمَ عَمَلِكَ.

I entrust to Allah your religion, your covenant and your final deeds.[2]

Nasā'ī and others record a variation of that hadith, where it is reported that he ﷺ would say,

إِذَا اسْتُودِعَ اللهُ شَيْئًا حَفِظَهُ.

Whenever Allah is entrusted with something, he safeguards it.[3]

Ṭabarānī records a [variation of this] hadith from the Prophet ﷺ:

إِنَّ الْعَبْدَ إِذَا صَلَّى الصَّلَاةَ عَلَى وَجْهِهَا صَعِدَتْ إِلَى اللهِ وَلَهَا بُرْهَانٌ كَبُرْهَانِ الشَّمْسِ وَتَقُولُ لِصَاحِبِهِ: حَفِظَكَ اللهُ كَمَا حَفِظْتَنِي، وَإِذَا ضَيَّعَهَا لُفَّتْ كَمَا يُلَفُّ الثَّوْبُ الْخَلِقُ، ثُمَّ يُضْرَبُ بِهَا وَجْهُ صَاحِبِهَا وَتَقُولُ لَهُ: ضَيَّعَكَ اللهُ كَمَا ضَيَّعْتَنِي.

When a slave [of Allah] offers the prayer as it should be offered, it ascends to Allah ﷻ with a proof as clear as the sun, saying to its owner, 'May Allah safeguard you as you were mindful of me!' And when he neglects it, it is rolled up like a shabby cloth and thrown back into the face of its owner, saying to him, 'May Allah neglect you as you neglected me!'[4]

1 Ibn Ḥibbān (934).
2 Tirmidhī (3443); Abū Dāwūd (2600); Ibn Mājah (2826); Aḥmad (4524).
3 Nasā'ī, *as-Sunan al-Kubrā* (10269); Aḥmad (5605).
4 Ṭabarānī (3095)

ʿUmar used to say when he addressed the people, 'O Allah! Guard us with you protection and make us firm upon Your command.'

Once, a man supplicated for one of the early Muslim, praying for his protection, but someone told him, 'O my brother! Do not ask for his protection. Rather, ask for the protection of his belief.' This means that supplicating for the protection of one's religion is more essential; both the righteous and the sinners partake in worldly protection, while Allah only safeguards a believer's religion. Allah bars any access to him, preventing harmful things from reaching him through certain means, some of which he is totally oblivious to and others which he, [in his ignorance] disapproves of. Allah safeguarded Yūsuf precisely in this way:

﴿كَذَٰلِكَ لِنَصْرِفَ عَنْهُ السُّوءَ وَالْفَحْشَاءَ إِنَّهُ مِنْ عِبَادِنَا الْمُخْلَصِينَ﴾

That happened so We might avert from him all evil and lust. He was Our chosen slave. (12:24)

Whoever is dedicated to Allah, He will purge him of all evil and lust, and protect him from them in ways which he knows not. Allah intervenes, coming between him and causes of damning sins. For example, Maʿrūf al-Karkhī saw some youngsters preparing to go out to fight during the civil strife, so he said, 'O Allah! Protect them.' When he was asked, 'Are you supplicating for these people?' he replied, '[I mean that Allah has not protected them, for if] If He had protected them, they would not have gone to do what they are intent on doing.'

ʿUmar once heard a man saying, 'O Allah! Indeed, You intervene between a person and his heart, so intervene between me and Your disobedience.' ʿUmar approved, supplicating to Allah to bless him with good.

It is related that Ibn ʿAbbās explained the words of Allah,

﴿وَاعْلَمُوا أَنَّ اللَّهَ يَحُولُ بَيْنَ الْمَرْءِ وَقَلْبِهِ﴾

Know that Allah intervenes between a man and his heart (8:24), 'He intervenes between believers and the disobedience which will drag them to the Fire.'

One of the early Muslims performed hajj and stayed with a group of people in Makkah. When he intended to commit a sin, a voice called out to him, 'Woe to you! Have you not just performed hajj?' Therefore, Allah ﷻ saved him from what he had intended.

Another one of the early Muslim proceeded with a group of people to commit a sin. When he was determined to carry out the act, someone called out,

﴿كُلُّ نَفْسٍ بِمَا كَسَبَتْ رَهِينَةٌ﴾

Every self is held in pledge against what it earned (74:38), so he abstained.

A man once entered a forest, thinking to himself, 'If I committed a sin here, in private, who will see me?' Then he heard a voice coming from every direction, saying:

﴿أَلَا يَعْلَمُ مَنْ خَلَقَ وَهُوَ اللَّطِيفُ الْخَبِيرُ﴾

Does He Who created not then know? He is the All-Pervading, the All-Aware. (67:14)

Another man was determined to commit a sin, so he set out to do it. On his way, he passed by a storyteller narrating to the people. He stopped at his circle and heard him saying, 'O one who intends to sin! Do you not know that the One Who created intention knows your intent?' He then fell unconscious, and when he regained consciousness, he repented immediately.

Another incident is that a certain pious king became fearful for himself when he became infatuated with a beautiful subject of his, so he stood one night in prayer and asked Allah ﷻ for help. The subject fell ill that night, dying three days later.

[HE ﷻ WILL PROTECT YOUR RELIGION THROUGH AN ACCOMPLICE]

Some slaves of Allah ﷻ were protected through a warning that manifested on the tongue of an accomplice in the sin, like the incident of the three who entered the cave and were trapped by the rock. [It is related that] when one of the three sat between a woman's legs, she said, 'Slave of Allah! Fear Allah and do not break the seal except with its due right,' so he left her.[1]

Similarly, there is the case of the guarantor from the Tribe of Isrā'īl who sinned persistently, as quoted by Imam Aḥmad and Tirmidhī in the hadith of Ibn 'Umar ﷺ from the Prophet ﷺ. It is related that he became fond of a woman, so he gave her sixty dinars [to have his way with her]. When he sat in position [ready to commit the act] she trembled with fear, prompting him to ask her, 'Have I forced you?' She replied, 'No, but I would never have done this act. Necessity has left me no choice but to do it.' He then said [regrettably], 'You fear Allah but I do not!' and he left her and gifted her the money. He said, 'By Allah, the guarantor shall never again disobey Allah.' He passed away that night, and in the morning, the following was written on his door: 'Allah has forgiven the guarantor.'[2]

Another man once attempted to seduce a woman, and when he told her to lock the doors, she did so and then said to him, 'Only one door remains.' He asked, 'Which door is that?' She replied, 'The door between us and Allah ﷻ.' At that moment, he turned away from her. Another man, while attempting to seduce a Bedouin woman, told her, 'No one can see us but the stars.' So she asked him, 'Then where is the Creator of the stars?'

All of these examples are from the kindness of Allah ﷻ and how He intercepts between a slave and his sin.

Ḥasan said when mentioning the sinful, 'They underestimated

1 Bukhārī (2215); Muslim (2743).

2 Aḥmad (4747); Tirmidhī (2496).

Allah, leading to them disobeyed Him. Had they realised His greatness, He would have protected them [from disobedience].'

Bishr once said, 'No person with a honour would persistently disobey Allah, and no wise person would ever prefer the world to the Hereafter.'

[HE WILL PROTECT YOU THROUGH INTERCEPTION]

Allah also safeguards His slave's religion by intercepting some worldly means, such as friendships, business and other such relationships. This is because Allah knows that there is good for him in that [interception], though he, begrudgingly, is unaware of it.

Ibn Masʿūd said,

> Sometimes, a slave of Allah is determined to carry out some business or he aspires to a position of authority, and he very nearly achieves it. Meanwhile, Allah watches him and says to the angels, 'Take it from him. If I facilitate this for him, I will enter him into the Fire.' So, Allah snatches that from him, while he assumes it to be bad luck, moaning, 'So-and-so surpassed me' and 'so-and-so is smarter than me,' but it is nothing but the bounty of Allah.

More amazing still is that sometimes, the slave of Allah wants to perform an act of obedience but there is no good in it for him, so Allah intervenes between him and that action in order to protect him, though he is unaware.

Ṭabarānī and others quote the hadith of Anas from the Prophet that Allah says,

> إِنَّ مِنْ عِبَادِي مَنْ لَا يُصْلِحُ إِيمَانَهُ إِلَّا الْفَقْرُ، وَلَوْ بَسَطْتُ عَلَيْهِ أَفْسَدَهُ ذَلِكَ، وَإِنَّ مِنْ عِبَادِي مَنْ لَا يُصْلِحُ إِيمَانَهُ إِلَّا الْغِنَى، وَلَوْ أَفْقَرْتُهُ لَأَفْسَدَهُ ذَلِكَ، وَإِنَّ مِنْ عِبَادِي مَنْ لَا يُصْلِحُ إِيمَانَهُ إِلَّا الصِّحَّةُ، وَلَوْ أَسْقَمْتُهُ لَأَفْسَدَهُ ذَلِكَ، وَإِنَّ مِنْ عِبَادِي مَنْ لَا يُصْلِحُ إِيمَانَهُ إِلَّا السَّقَمُ، وَلَوْ صَحَّحْتُهُ لَأَفْسَدَهُ ذَلِكَ، وَإِنَّ مِنْ عِبَادِي مَنْ يَطْلُبُ بَابًا مِنَ الْعِبَادَةِ فَأَكُفُّهُ عَنْهُ لِكَيْلَا يَدْخُلَهُ

الْعُجْبُ، إِنِّي أُدَبِّرُ عِبَادِي بِعِلْمِي بِمَا فِي قُلُوبِهِمْ، إِنِّي عَلِيمٌ خَبِيرٌ.

> The only thing suitable for the belief of some of My slaves is poverty; and if I were to give them in abundance, it would corrupt them. For others, the only thing suitable for their belief is wealth; and if I were to impoverish them, it would spoil them. For some, the only thing suitable for their belief is health; and if I were to make them sick, it would ruin them. And for others, the only thing suitable for their belief is sickness; and if I were to cure them, it would pervert them. Some of My slaves intend to do a specific worship, but I prevent him, so that pride does not overtake him. I manage My slaves with My knowledge according to what is in their hearts. I am All-Knowing All-Aware.[1]

One of the early Muslims used to persistently ask for martyrdom, when a voice called out to him, 'If you were to fight, you would be imprisoned, and if you were to be imprisoned, you would become a Christian.' He never asked for martyrdom thereafter.

To summarise, whoever is mindful of the limits of Allah ﷻ and guards His rights, Allah ﷻ will take charge of protecting his religious and worldly matters in this world and the Hereafter. Allah ﷻ says in His Book that He is the protector of the believers and that He Himself will take charge of the righteous, including managing their worldly and other-worldly interests.

Allah ﷻ says,

﴿اللَّهُ وَلِيُّ الَّذِينَ آمَنُوا﴾

Allah is the protector of those who believe. (2:257)

And He ﷻ says,

﴿ذَلِكَ بِأَنَّ اللَّهَ مَوْلَى الَّذِينَ آمَنُوا وَأَنَّ الْكَافِرِينَ لَا مَوْلَى لَهُمْ﴾

That is because Allah is the protector of those who believe and because those who disbelieve have no protector. (47:11)

He ﷻ also says,

1 Bayhaqī, *al-Asmā' wa 'ṣ-Ṣifāt* (231); Ibn Abī 'd-Dunyā, *Awliyā'* (1).

﴿وَمَن يَتَوَكَّلْ عَلَى اللَّهِ فَهُوَ حَسْبُهُ﴾

Whoever puts his trust in Allah, He will be enough for him. (65:3)

And He ﷻ says,

﴿أَلَيْسَ اللَّهُ بِكَافٍ عَبْدَهُ﴾

Is Allah not enough for His slave? (39:36)

If an individual upholds the rights of Allah ﷻ, He ﷻ will surely take responsibility for him, tending to all of his interests in the world and the Hereafter. So whoever wants Allah ﷻ to personally protect him and keep him safe in all his matters should first consider Allah's rights over him. Similarly, whoever wishes to be safe from what he dislikes should not do anything that Allah ﷻ dislikes for him.

One of the early Muslims would pass by gatherings saying, 'Whoever wishes for perpetual well-being should fear Allah ﷻ.'

Someone once asked ʿUmrī the Ascetic for advice, so he said, 'Be with Allah ﷻ as you would love Allah to be with you.'

Ṣāliḥ ibn ʿAbd al-Karīm said, 'Allah ﷻ says, "By my honour and my majesty, when I peer into the heart of a slave whom I know loves to hold fast to My obedience, I manage his responsibilities and his conduct."'

Some of the earlier Books have recorded that Allah ﷻ says, 'Son of Ādam! Will you not tell Me what makes you laugh? Son of Ādam! Fear me and sleep peacefully wherever you wish.' This means that, if you uphold the rights of fearing Allah ﷻ, which He has over you, you need not be concerned with any affairs beyond that. Allah ﷻ knows your interests better than you do, and He will bring them to you in the most perfect way without you having to worry about them.

It is mentioned in the hadith of Jābir ؓ from the Prophet ﷺ,

مَنْ كَانَ يُحِبُّ أَنْ يَعْلَمَ مَنْزِلَتَهُ عِنْدَ اللهِ فَلْيَنْظُرْ كَيْفَ مَنْزِلَةُ اللهِ عِنْدَهُ، فَإِنَّ اللهَ يُنْزِلُ الْعَبْدَ مِنْهُ حَيْثُ أَنْزَلَهُ مِنْ نَفْسِهِ.

Whoever wishes to know his position in the sight of Allah ﷻ

> should consider Allah's position in his conduct. Allah ﷻ grants His slave a position with Him according to the position he has set for Allah.[1]

This shows that Allah's ﷻ care and safeguarding of His slave will be commensurate to His slave's concern for Him ﷻ, his implementation and consideration of His limits and how mindful he is of Allah ﷻ. Whoever's greatest concern is the pleasure of Allah ﷻ and seeking His proximity, His recognition, His love and servitude to Him, Allah will treat him accordingly, as He ﷻ says,

﴿فَاذْكُرُونِي أَذْكُرْكُمْ﴾

Remember Me, I will remember you. (2:152)

And He ﷻ says,

﴿وَأَوْفُوا بِعَهْدِي أُوفِ بِعَهْدِكُمْ﴾

Honour My contract and I will honour your contract. (2:40)

In fact, He ﷻ is the Most Generous of those who show generosity, for He rewards a single good deed with tenfold and even more! Whoever advances to Him by a hand span, He ﷻ will advance to him by a cubit; and whoever advances to Him by a cubit, He ﷻ will advance to him by a fathom; and whoever comes to Him walking, He ﷻ will go to him running.

[Good or bad,] whatever man receives is from himself. If he is afflicted by a calamity, it is because he transgressed the limits of his Lord ﷻ. It is as ʿAlī ﷺ said, 'A slave should hope for nothing except his Lord and should fear nothing except his sins.'

One of the scholars said, 'Whoever devotes himself will be devoted to; and whoever is confounded will remain confused.' Masrūq said, 'Whoever is mindful of Allah ﷻ when his perilous thoughts get the better of his heart, Allah ﷻ will protect the movement of his limbs.' Expounding the meaning of this will be very lengthy and what we have touched on will suffice. All praise is for Allah ﷻ.

1 Ṭabarānī, *Awsaṭ* (2501).

CHAPTER 3

Be Mindful of Allah ﷻ and You Will Find Him in Front of You

In another variation, the hadith says, 'Be mindful of Allah and you will find Him facing you.'[1] This means that the one who is mindful of the limits of Allah ﷻ, upholding His rights will find Allah ﷻ encompassing him, helping him, safeguarding him, facilitating him, aiding him and correcting him in every situation. He is aware of every soul, seeing everything it does; and He ﷻ is with those who are righteous and God-fearing.

Qatādah said, 'Whoever fears Allah ﷻ, He is with him; and whoever has Allah ﷻ with him possesses a group that cannot be defeated, a guard that does not sleep and a guide that does not stray.'

One of the early Muslims wrote to his brother, 'As to what follows: If Allah ﷻ is with you, then who do you have to fear? If Allah ﷻ is against you, then what hope could you ever have? Peace be upon you.' This special union of the God-fearing with Allah ﷻ is not like the general 'being with' mentioned in His words:

﴿وَهُوَ مَعَكُمْ أَيْنَ مَا كُنتُمْ﴾

He is with you wherever you are (57:4)

---

1 Aḥmad (2763).

And,

﴿وَلَا يَسْتَخْفُونَ مِنَ اللهِ وَهُوَ مَعَهُمْ إِذْ يُبَيِّتُونَ﴾

They cannot conceal themselves from Allah. He is with them when they spend the night. (4:108)

The exclusive union includes assistance, aid, safeguarding and help, as He ﷻ said to Mūsā and Hārūn ﷺ,

﴿لَا تَخَافَا إِنَّنِي مَعَكُمَا أَسْمَعُ وَأَرَى﴾

Have no fear. I will be with you. (20:46)

And as He ﷻ said,

﴿إِذْ يَقُولُ لِصَاحِبِهِ لَا تَحْزَنْ إِنَّ اللهَ مَعَنَا﴾

He said to his companion, 'Do not be despondent, Allah is with us.' (9:40)

On the occasion referred to in the latter, the Prophet ﷺ said to Abū Bakr aṣ-Ṣiddīq ؓ,

مَا ظَنُّكَ بِاثْنَيْنِ اللهُ ثَالِثُهُمَا؟

What do you think will happen to the two, the third of whom is Allah?[1]

This does not have the same meaning as His words,

﴿مَا يَكُونُ مِنْ نَجْوَى ثَلَاثَةٍ إِلَّا هُوَ رَابِعُهُمْ﴾

Three men cannot confer together secretly without Him being the fourth of them (58:7), which applies generally to all groups of people.

We find an example of the special union, from the words of Allah ﷻ, as mentioned in a hadith:

وَلَا يَزَالُ عَبْدِي يَتَقَرَّبُ إِلَيَّ بِالنَّوَافِلِ حَتَّى أُحِبَّهُ، فَإِذَا أَحْبَبْتُهُ، كُنْتُ سَمْعَهُ الَّذِي يَسْمَعُ بِهِ، وَبَصَرَهُ الَّذِي يُبْصِرُ بِهِ، وَيَدَهُ الَّتِي يَبْطِشُ بِهَا، وَرِجْلَهُ الَّتِي يَمْشِي بِهَا.

1 Bukhārī (4663).

> My slave continues to draw closer to Me through supererogatory acts of worship until I love him. Then when I love him, I become his hearing through which he hears, his sight through which he sees, his hand with which he strikes and his leg with which walks.[1]

This and many other texts from the Qur'an and the Sunnah indicate the Lord's ﷻ proximity to the one who obeys and fears Him, and is mindful of His limits and upholds them.

Once, on the way to Tabuk, Bunān al-Ḥammāl passed through a desert. He began to feel lonely and so a caller called out to him, 'Why do you feel lonely? Is your Beloved not with you?'

This shows that whoever is mindful of Allah ﷻ and upholds His rights will find Him right there front of him in every situation. So take Him as your companion and be satisfied with Him, and dispense with all need for creation.

It is mentioned in a hadith, as recorded by Ṭabarānī and others,

أَفْضَلُ الْإِيمَانِ أَن يَعْلَمَ الْعَبْدُ أَنَّ اللهَ مَعَهُ حَيْثُمَا كَانَ.

> 'The best faith is knowing that Allah ﷻ is with you wherever you are.'[2] Again, elaborating on this hadith would prove very lengthy, [so we suffice on this brief discussion].

One righteous scholar would frequently travel alone. On one occasion, the people came out to bid him farewell, but he sent them back, saying,

> When we set out as night falls and You are in front of us,
> Your remembrance suffices as a guide for our mounts.

Shiblī used to recite this couplet, and sometimes, the gathering would have to be stopped [because of the effect it had on him and the audience].

---

1 Bukhārī (6502).

2 Ṭabarānī, *Awsaṭ* (8796); Abū Nuʿaym, *Ḥilyah* (6:124).

CHAPTER 4

Become Acquainted with Allah ﷻ in Times of Ease and He Will Recognise You in Times of Hardship

This means that if the slave of Allah ﷻ fears Him and is mindful of His limits and upholds His rights in times of ease and health, then through that he has become acquainted with Allah ﷻ. Hence, his Lord will recognise him in times of difficulty, acknowledging his deeds in times of ease, and save him from all hardships on the strength of that acquaintance.

This is also a special acquaintance, which includes the proximity of Allah ﷻ, His love and His acceptance of supplications, and it does not refer to mere general recognition. Allah ﷻ knows and recognises the condition of every one of His creation, as He says,

﴿هُوَ أَعْلَمُ بِكُمْ إِذْ أَنْشَأَكُمْ مِنَ الْأَرْضِ وَإِذْ أَنْتُمْ أَجِنَّةٌ فِي بُطُونِ أُمَّهَاتِكُمْ﴾

He has most knowledge of you when He first produced you from the earth, and when you were embryos in your mothers' wombs. (53:32)

And He ﷻ says,

﴿وَلَقَدْ خَلَقْنَا الْإِنْسَانَ وَنَعْلَمُ مَا تُوَسْوِسُ بِهِ نَفْسُهُ﴾

We created man and We know what his own self whispers to him. (50:16)

However, what Allah ﷻ refers to in the hadith: 'My slave continues to draw closer to me through supererogatory acts of worship until I love him. . .' until His words 'If he asks of Me, I will surely give him; and if he seeks refuge in Me, I will surely grant him refuge,' is a specific personal acquaintance.[1]

Fuḍayl once met Sha'wānah the Worshipper and asked her to pray for him. She replied, 'Fuḍayl! What is the problem between you and Him? [Why can you not ask him yourself?] If you pray to Him, He will respond to you.' So Fuḍayl sobbed profusely and fell unconscious.

Abū Jaʿfar as-Sā'iḥ said,

> Ḥasan, fleeing from Ḥajjāj, came to Ḥabīb Abū Muhammad. He said to him, 'Abū Muhammad! Save me from the authorities, as they are on my tail.' He responded, 'I am embarrassed for you, Abū Saʿīd! Is there no reliance between you and your Lord, whereby you can supplicate to Him and He will hide you from them? Enter the house.' When the authorities entered after him, they could not see him. Later, when they told Ḥajjāj what happened, he said, 'He was definitely in the house, but Allah obscured their sight so they could not see him.'

When the slave of Allah ﷻ attains this special recognition, he gains special acquaintance with his Lord ﷻ; not the general recognition of the masses, but the recognition which leads to friendship with Him and prompts him to act modestly in front of him. Gaining this acquaintance and recognition has been the driving force for all gnostics, as can be gleaned from their allusions [in many an incident]. Abū Sulaymān heard a man once say, 'I spent the night talking about women.' So he reprimanded him, 'Woe to you! Have you no shame before Him? He ﷻ sees you talking about someone other than Him at night. But how can you have shame before the One Whom you have yet to recognise?' Aḥmad ibn ʿĀṣim al-Anṭākī said, 'I do not want to die until I have recognised my Lord. Recognition of Him

1 Bukhārī (6502).

is not just affirming Him; but recognising Him is to have shame in front of Him.'

This special recognition and acquaintance creates peace of mind and certainty that Allah ﷻ will surely save him from every hardship and calamity. This acquaintance also means that the Lord will accept the supplication of His slave. When Ḥasan hid from Ḥajjāj, someone advised him, 'You should leave Basrah; we fear you will be discovered.' This made him weep, and he said, 'Should I leave my city, my family and my brothers? My acquaintance with my Lord and His blessings upon me show me that He ﷻ will save me and free me from them, if Allah ﷻ wills.' Accordingly, Ḥajjāj did not harm him at all; rather, he would honour him greatly after that and would always speak positively about him.

A man once said to Maʿrūf, 'What has stirred you to sever all ties and devote to worship?' The man then listed death, the Barrier between this life and the next, Paradise and the Fire [and asked if any of these motivated him], but Maʿrūf said, 'What are these?! The King possesses all of these in His hand. If there was recognition between you and Him, He would suffice you against all of these!'

Tirmidhī quotes a hadith from Abū Hurayrah ؓ, which clarifies and explains this, that the Prophet ﷺ said,

مَنْ سَرَّهُ أَنْ يَسْتَجِيبَ اللهُ لَهُ عِنْدَ الشَّدَائِدِ فَلْيُكْثِرِ الدُّعَاءَ فِي الرَّخَاءِ.

'Whoever wants Allah to accept his supplication at the time of hardship should increase supplication at times of ease.'[1] Ibn Abī 'd-Dunyā, Ibn Abī Ḥātim, Ibn Jarīr and others quote the hadith of Yazīd ar-Raqqāshī from Anas ؓ, who relates from the Prophet ﷺ,

أَنَّ يُونُسَ عَلَيْهِ السَّلَام دَعَا وَهُوَ فِي بَطْنِ الحُوتِ، قَالَتِ المَلائِكَةُ: يَا رَبِّ هَذَا صَوْتٌ مَعْرُوفٌ فِي بِلادٍ غَرِيبَةٍ، قَالَ: أَمَا تَعْرِفُونَ ذلكَ؟ قَالُوا: وَمَنْ هُوَ؟ قَالَ: عَبْدِي يُونُسُ، قَالُوا: عَبْدُكَ يُونُسُ الَّذِي لَمْ يَزَلْ يُرْفَعُ لَهُ عَمَلٌ

1 Tirmidhī relates a variation of this hadith (3382).

مُتَقَبَّلٌ وَدَعْوَةٌ مُسْتَجَابَةٌ؟ قَالَ: نَعَمْ، قَالُوا: يَا رَبِّ، أَفَلَا تَرْحَمُ مَا كَانَ يَصْنَعُ فِي الرَّخَاءِ فَتُنْجِيَهُ مِنَ البَلَاءِ؟ قَالَ: بَلَى، فَأَمَرَ اللهُ الْحُوتَ فَطَرَحَهُ بِالعَرَاءِ.

When Yūnus supplicated to Allah while in the belly of the whale, the angels said, 'Our Lord! This is a familiar voice coming from a strange place!' So Allah said, 'Do you not know who that is?' They asked, 'Who is he?' Allah responded, 'My slave, Yūnus.' The angels said, 'Your slave, Yūnus, the one whose accepted deeds and answered supplications continue to ascend to the heavens?' Allah said, 'Yes.' The angels said, 'Will You not then have mercy, because of what he used to do in times of ease, and save him from hardship?' Allah said, 'Of course.' Then He ordered the whale to cast him up on to the beach.[1]

Ḍaḥḥāk ibn Qays said,

> Remember Allah in times of ease and He will remember you in times of hardship. Yūnus used to remember Allah [in times of ease], then when he was in the belly of the whale, Allah said,
>
> ﴿فَلَوْلَا أَنَّهُ كَانَ مِنَ الْمُسَبِّحِينَ ۝١٤٣ لَلَبِثَ فِي بَطْنِهِ إِلَى يَوْمِ يُبْعَثُونَ ۝١٤٤﴾
>
> *Had it not been that he was a man who glorified Allah, he would have remained inside its belly.* (37:143–144)
>
> Moreover, Firʿawn rebelled and forgot about the remembrance of Allah. Then when he was drowning he said, 'I believe.' Allah said,
>
> ﴿آلْآنَ وَقَدْ عَصَيْتَ قَبْلُ وَكُنْتَ مِنَ الْمُفْسِدِينَ﴾
>
> *'What, now? When previously you rebelled and were one of the corrupters?'* (10:91)

Rishdīn ibn Saʿd said, 'A man said to Abū 'd-Dardā', "Give me

1 Ibn Abī 'd-Dunyā, *al-Faraj baʿd ash-Shiddah* (32); Ibn Abī Ḥātim (13710); Ṭabarī (21:109).

counsel." So he said, "Remember Allah in times of ease and He will remember you in times of hardship."'

Salmān al-Fārisī ﷺ said,

> If a man usually supplicates in times of ease, then when hardship befalls him and he supplicates to Allah ﷻ, the angels will say, 'A familiar voice,' and they will intercede for him. But if he was not accustomed to supplicating in times of ease, and hardship befalls him and he supplicates to Allah ﷻ, the angels will say, 'An unfamiliar voice,' and they do not intercede for him.

The hadith of the three who entered the cave, only to be trapped by a boulder bears testimony to this too. They were helped because of their supplication to Allah ﷻ through the means of sincere deeds that they had performed in times of ease, such as being dutiful to parents, forsaking fornication and fulfilling a hidden trust.[1]

[PREPARATION FOR DEATH]

Once it is known that becoming acquainted with Allah ﷻ in times of ease necessitates Allah's recognition of His slave in times of hardship, then there is no greater hardship facing a believer than death. Death is insignificant compared to what follows, if the slave's destined place of return is the evil abode; and if his final abode is good, then it will be the last hardship he ever faces.

The slave of Allah ﷻ must, therefore, prepare for death with righteous deeds, rushing to perform them before it comes. Indeed, a person does not know at what time of the day or night this hardship will afflict him.

One of the ways the hardship of death is lightened and hope is restored is through recounting past righteous deeds, improving a believer's opinion about Allah ﷻ. One of the early Muslims said, 'The pious loved to prepare a hoard of righteous deeds to facilitate ease

1 Bukhārī (2272).

when death comes' or something to that effect. They also saw it as an amazing achievement when someone died immediately after doing an act of obedience, like hajj, jihad or fasting.

Nakhaʿī said, 'People used to recommend recounting a person's righteous deeds at the time of his death so that he would be optimistic about Allah ﷻ.'

Abū ʿAbd ar-Raḥmān as-Sulamī said, when he was sick, 'How can I not have hope in Allah ﷻ when I have fasted eighty Ramadans?'

When death approached Abū Bakr ibn ʿAyyāsh, the people around him wept, so he said, 'Do not weep. I have completed the Qur'an in this prayer room 13,000 times.' He is also related to have said to his son, 'Do you think Allah ﷻ would waste the forty years your father completed the Qur'an every night?'

When death approached one of the early Muslims, he said to his son when he saw him weeping, 'Do not weep, for your father has never done an immoral act.'

Ādam ibn Abī Iyās completed the Qur'an while he was laying on his death bed, then he said, 'By my love for You, be gentle with me in this fatal encounter. I have had expectations of You for this day and I have high hopes in You. There is no God but Allah.' Then he passed away, may Allah ﷻ have mercy on him.

ʿAbd aṣ-Ṣamad the Ascetic would say at the time of his death, 'My Master! For this moment I have held on to You, and this day I have gained You. Please confirm my good opinion of You.'

Ibn ʿAqīl said at the time of his death, while women wept, 'For fifty years, I have been working for Him. Leave me so I can enjoy my meeting with Him.'

When the Qarāmiṭah[1] attacked the pilgrims, killing them while they made *ṭawāf*, ʿAlī ibn Bābawayh the Sufi did not stop his circumambulation, even though swords were striking him until he fell. He then recited,

---

1 The Qarāmiṭah were a ninth-century Shīʿī sect who rebelled against the Abbasid Caliphate. They attacked Makkah during the hajj, stole the Black Stone and desecrated the Well of Zamzam with the bodies of dead pilgrims.

You see the lovers going mad in their homes
Like the youngsters of the cave, not knowing how long they tarried.

He then recited another couplet:

By Allah, had the lovers sworn that they would die
Because of disunion on the day of discord, they would not be lying.

Whoever obeys Allah ﷻ and fears Him and is mindful of His limits, Allah will take charge of him at the time of his death. He ﷻ will cause him to die on belief and will reinforce him with the firm word in the grave when the angels question him. He ﷻ will then protect him from the punishment of the grave and ease his loneliness in that dark desolation. One of the early Muslims said, 'If Allah ﷻ is with you when you enter the grave, then no harm will come to you and you will not be lonely.'

When a certain righteous scholars was seen in a dream after his death and asked about what happened to him, he replied, 'My Lord ﷻ befriended me.' It is hoped that whoever befriends Allah ﷻ in seclusion in the world, Allah ﷻ will befriend him in the darkness of the grave when he parts from the world.

One of the pious early Muslims said, to this effect,

So, my Lord! Befriend me on the day of my loneliness,
For I surely affirm what You have revealed.
I am not worried that I must go to Allah;
who from my family could be more devoted and friendlier than Him.

The aforementioned also relates to the horrors, fears and hardships of the Day of Rising: if Allah ﷻ takes charge of a slave who is obedient to Him in the world, He ﷻ will save him from all of that.

Qatādah explained the words of Allah ﷻ:

﴿وَمَنْ يَتَّقِ اللَّهَ يَجْعَل لَّهُ مَخْرَجًا﴾

Whoever fears Allah, He will give him a way out (65:2), '[Such a person will be given a way out] from the troubles of death and the fears of the Day of Rising.' ʿAlī ibn Abī Ṭalḥah relates that Ibn ʿAbbās ﷺ said it means, 'We will save him from every worry in this world and the Hereafter.'

Zayd ibn Aslam said regarding Allah's ﷻ words,

﴿إِنَّ الَّذِينَ قَالُوا رَبُّنَا اللَّهُ ثُمَّ اسْتَقَامُوا﴾

Those who say, 'Our Lord is Allah,' and then go straight (46:13), 'He will be given glad tidings of that at the time of his death, in his grave and on the Day he is raised up. He will have entered the Garden, but the elation he felt from the glad tidings will still remain in his heart.' Ibn Abī Ḥātim and others have quoted that Thābit al-Bunānī said regarding the same verse,

> It has reached us that when Allah ﷻ raises a believer from his grave, the two angels who were with him in the world will meet him and say, 'Do not fear and do not grieve.' Allah ﷻ will relieve him of his fear and delight him. Any calamity that descends upon the people on the Day of Rising will be nothing but pleasure for the believer, because Allah ﷻ guided him and because of his deeds in the world.

As for the one who does not recognise Allah ﷻ in times of ease, there will be no one to look out for him in times of hardship, neither in the world nor the Hereafter. The miserable fate of such people has been witnessed first-hand in the world, and yet, their state in the Hereafter will be far worse, as they will have no protector nor helper there.

CHAPTER 5

When You Ask, Ask Allah ﷻ

The Prophet ﷺ commanded us to ask Allah ﷻ alone and prohibited us from asking anyone other than Him. Allah ﷻ commanded us to ask of Him,

﴿وَاسْأَلُوا اللَّهَ مِنْ فَضْلِهِ﴾

But ask Allah for His bounty. (4:32)

Tirmidhī quotes from Ibn Masʿūd ؓ that the Prophet ﷺ said,

سَلُوا اللَّهَ مِنْ فَضْلِهِ، فَإِنَّ اللَّهَ يُحِبُّ أَنْ يُسْأَلَ.

Ask Allah for His bounty because Allah loves to be asked.[1]

He also quotes from Abū Hurayrah ؓ that the Prophet ﷺ said,

إِنَّ اللَّهَ يُحِبُّ الْمُلِحِّينَ فِي الدُّعَاءِ.

Allah loves those who beseech earnestly in supplication.[2]

In another hadith, it states,

لِيَسْأَلْ أَحَدُكُمْ رَبَّهُ حَاجَتَهُ كُلَّهَا حَتَّى يَسْأَلَ شِسْعَ نَعْلِهِ إِذَا انْقَطَعَ.

1 Tirmidhī (3571).

2 Ṭabarānī, *Duʿāʾ* (20).

> Every one of you should ask his Lord for all his needs; even asking for a strap for his shoe when it breaks.[1]

There are many hadiths with a similar meaning and there are numerous authentic hadiths prohibiting asking from creation.

In the hadith of Ibn Masʿūd رضي الله عنه, the Prophet ﷺ said,

لَا يَزَالُ الْعَبْدُ يَسْأَلُ وَهُوَ غَنِيٌّ حَتَّى يَخْلُقَ وَجْهُهُ فَمَا يَكُونُ لَهُ عِنْدَ اللهِ وَجْهٌ

> The slave of Allah ﷻ continues to ask [people for things], though he does not need to, until his reputation is worn out. Then, he has no honour in the sight of Allah ﷻ.[2]

The Prophet ﷺ took a pledge from a group of Companions that they would not ask people for anything. This group included Abū Bakr aṣ-Ṣiddīq, Abū Dharr and Thawbān رضي الله عنهم. If any of them dropped his whip or his camel's halter, he would not even ask anyone to hand it to him.[3]

[JUSTIFICATION FOR ONLY ASKING ALLAH ﷻ]

Asking Allah ﷻ and not His creation is justified logically, and according to the Sharīʿah, for a number of reasons. For instance, because asking compromises one's honour and is degrading for him, it should not be done for anyone except Allah ﷻ alone. An individual should not humble himself through worship and asking before anyone but Allah ﷻ. This is a true sign of love.

Yūsuf ibn al-Ḥusayn was asked, 'What is wrong with the lovers who take pleasure at their degradation in love?' So he recited,

> Degradation of the young man for love is most welcome,
> And humbling himself before his Beloved is an honour.

---

1 Tirmidhī (3604)

2 Abū Nuʿaym relates a variation of this hadith in *Ḥilyah* (2:21); Ṭabarānī, *Kabīr* has *yaḥliqu* instead of *yakhluqu* (790).

3 Muslim (1043).

This degradation and love is only suitable for Allah ﷻ alone; it is the true worship, exclusive only to the True God.

Imam Aḥmad used to say in his supplication, 'O Allah! Save my face from asking anyone other than You, just as You have saved it from prostrating to anyone other than You.'

Abū 'l-Khayr al-Aqṭaʿ said,

> I was in Makkah for a year when hardship and poverty befell me. Whenever I wanted to go out to ask from people, a voice would cry out, 'You wish to sacrifice the honour of the face you prostrate to Me on for someone other than Me?'

Similarly, one of the early Muslims would say,

> Sacrificing one's honour by asking begets no compensation,
> Even though wealth is acquired through asking.
> Were you to weigh the worth of asking against favours,
> Asking would prove weightier and every favour light.
> If you must sacrifice your honour through asking,
> Then only surrender it to the Most Kind, Most Generous.

The punishment of the one who persistently asks people without need will reflect this degradation. On the Day of Rising, his face will have no shred of flesh, as is established in the *Ṣaḥīḥayn*.[1] He has wasted his honour and integrity in the world, so, in the Hereafter, Allah ﷻ takes away the tangible beauty and splendour of his face, leaving it a mere skull will no flesh. Allah ﷻ also takes away his metaphorical beauty and splendour, leaving him bereft of honour in the sight of Allah ﷻ.

[ASKING ALLAH ﷻ IS WORSHIP]

Another reason why one should only ask from Allah ﷻ is that asking is a great form of worship, since it displays neediness towards Him and acknowledgement of His power to fulfil needs. Asking creation

1 Bukhārī (1474); Muslim (103).

is an injustice, since created beings are incapable of gaining benefit and removing harm for themselves, let alone extend the same to others! By asking them, you incorrectly assign to them the position of someone who has capability.

A hadith in the *Ṣaḥīḥ* of Muslim from Abū Dharr ﵁, who quotes from the Prophet ﷺ, confirms this meaning:

> يَا عِبَادِي، لَوْ أَنَّ أَوَّلَكُمْ وَآخِرَكُمْ وَإِنْسَكُمْ وَجِنَّكُمْ قَامُوا فِي صَعِيدٍ وَاحِدٍ فَسَأَلُونِي فَأَعْطَيْتُ كُلَّ إِنْسَانٍ مَسْأَلَتَهُ، مَا نَقَصَ ذَلِكَ مِمَّا عِنْدِي إِلَّا كَمَا يَنْقُصُ الْمِخْيَطُ إِذَا أُدْخِلَ الْبَحْرَ.
>
> My slaves! If the first of you and the last of you, your humans and your jinn, were to stand on one plain and ask Me and I were to give every person what he asked for, it would not decrease what I possess, except like the amount a needle takes from the sea when it is dipped in it.'[1]

In Tirmidhī and other books there is the following addition to the hadith:

> ذَلِكَ بِأَنِّي جَوَادٌ وَاجِدٌ مَاجِدٌ أَفْعَلُ مَا أُرِيْدُ، عَطَائِي كَلَامٌ وَعَذَابِي كَلَامٌ، إِذَا أَرَدْتُ شَيْئًا فَإِنَّمَا أَقُولُ لَهُ: كُنْ، فَيَكُونُ.
>
> That is because I am the Generous, the Perceiver, the Glorious and I do what I will. My granting is but a word and My punishment is but a word. When I wish a thing I merely say to it 'Be!' and it is.[2]

How can one ask the poor, incapable one and leave the Need-free, the All-Powerful? This is completely absurd!

One of the early Muslims said, 'How can I ask for the world from one (created being) who does not own it, when I am ashamed to ask Allah ﷻ, its true owner, for it.

1 Muslim (2577).

2 Tirmidhī (2495); Aḥmad (21540).

Another early Muslim became extremely impoverished, and he decided to request assistance from one of his brothers. One night, however, he saw a dream of someone saying to him, 'Is it fitting for a free seeker's heart to incline towards slaves when Allah ﷻ possesses what he seeks?' When he awoke, his heart felt completely need-free.

One from the early pious Muslims said,

> I have read in one of the revealed scriptures that Allah ﷻ says:
>
> In times of difficulty, he has hopes in someone other than Me, but hardships are in My hand and I am the Living, the Self-Sustaining. Early in the morning, he has hopes in someone other than me, knocking at their doors, but the keys of the treasures are in My hand and My door is open to all who call Me. Is there anyone who raised his hopes in Me in his misfortune and I deprived him? Is there anyone who raised his hopes in Me in a calamity and I deprived him? Is there anyone who knocked on My door and I did not open it for him? I am the highest of all hopes, so how can I deprive hopes in Me? Am I a miser so that My slave becomes miserly with Me? Do the world, the Hereafter, honour and grace not belong to Me? Then what prevents the hopeful from raising hopes in Me? If I was to gather the inhabitants of the heavens and the earth and give every one of them everything, and I was to make every one of their hopes come true, it would not decrease My dominion to the amount of part of an ant. How can the dominion decrease when I am its Sustainer? Oh how wretched are those who despair from My mercy! Oh how wretched are those who disobey Me and rush to what I have forbidden!

[ALLAH ﷻ LOVES BEING ASKED]

Another reason for asking Allah ﷻ alone is that He loves to be asked and is angry with those who do not ask of Him. Allah ﷻ wants His slaves to incline towards Him, to ask of Him, to supplicate to Him and to need Him, and He ﷻ loves those who beseech Him earnestly in supplication.

As for created beings, most of them do not appreciate being asked because of their own poverty and incapacity. Ibn as-Sammāk said, 'Do not ask of the one who flees from you. Rather, ask of the One who commands you to ask Him.'

Abū 'l-ʿAtāhiyyah said,

Allah is angered if you stop asking Him,
    Whereas the children of Ādam are angered when you ask them.
So make your requests only to God,
    It is in the bounty of our Lord's favour that we live comfortably.

Yaḥyā ibn Muʿādh used to say, 'O One who is angered at those who do not ask You! Do not refuse the one who has asked you.'

One of the Bedouins recited:

O Mālik! Do not ask of people, but search for yourself!
    Allah's bounty is sufficient for you, for Allah is the Most Generous.
If man was asked for dust he would complain,
    And if it is said, 'Give!' he becomes weary and refuses.

[ALLAH ﷻ ASKS YOU TO ASK HIM]

Yet another reason for only asking Allah ﷻ is that He ﷻ asks His slaves to ask Him, and He calls out to them every night, 'Is there anyone who is asking that I may give him? Is there anyone who is supplicating that I may accept his request for him?'[1] Allah ﷻ says,

﴿وَإِذَا سَأَلَكَ عِبَادِى عَنِّى فَإِنِّى قَرِيبٌ أُجِيبُ دَعْوَةَ الدَّاعِ إِذَا دَعَانِ﴾

If My slaves ask you about Me, I am near. I answer the call of the caller when he calls on Me. (2:186)

Any time the slave calls Him, he will find Him to be the All-Hearing,

1 Muslim (758).

the Near and the One who responds, with no veil nor doorkeeper between him and Allah ﷻ. Created beings, on the other hand, use veils and doors to refuse those who ask, and most of the time, it is extremely difficult to even get close to them.

Ṭāwūs once said to ʿAṭā', 'Beware of seeking your needs from one who will close his door on you and hang a veil over it. Ask from the One whose door remains open until the Day of Rising. He has commanded you to ask Him and has promised to answer you.'

Wahb ibn Munabbih said to a scholar,

> Is it true that you go to kings and princes, carrying your knowledge to them? Woe to you! You go to one who will close his door on you, displaying his poverty to you and concealing his wealth from you. And you leave the One who opens His door for you in the middle of the night and the middle of the day, displaying His wealth to you. He ﷻ says,

﴿وَقَالَ رَبُّكُمُ ادْعُونِي أَسْتَجِبْ لَكُمْ﴾

Call on Me and I will answer you. (40:60)

Maymūn ibn Mihrān once saw some people gathered at the door of a leader, so he said, '[I say to] whoever has a need with the Sultan, who has screened himself, that indeed the houses of the All-Merciful are open. He should go the masjid, offer two units of prayer and ask for his need.'

Bakr al-Muzanī used to say, 'Who is like you, son of Ādam? Whenever you want you can purify yourself, then whisper to your Lord with no veil nor interpreter between you and Him.'

Someone once asked a righteous man to intercede on his behalf with another man regarding a need, so he said, 'I will not leave an open door to go to a closed door.'

With a similar meaning, one of the early Muslims said,

The courtyards of the kings are veiled
    While Allah's door is a generous veranda.

Another said,

> Say to those whom the needy cannot access,
> Because of houses where there are veils,
> 'If your doorkeeper intercepts those who wish to meet you,
> Then [know] there is no doorkeeper at Allah's door.'

One of the scholars said,

> Never sit at the door of the one
> Who refuses to let you enter his house.
> You say, 'My need is with him.
> He will withhold it if I do not wander around him.'
> Leave him and head for its Lord,
> It will be fulfilled in spite of the housekeeper.

Ibn Abī 'd-Dunyā quotes a hadith from Abū ʿUbaydah, son of ʿAbdullāh ibn Masʿūd, that a man came to the Prophet and said, 'Messenger of Allah! Such-and-such tribe deceived me and took off with my son and my camels.' The Prophet said to him, 'The family of Muhammad are like this and like that; people of a household who have no *mudd* or *ṣāʿ*[1] of food, so ask Allah.' So he returned to his wife, who asked, 'What did he say to you?' He informed her, so she said, 'Good is the response he gave you.' It was not long before Allah returned his son to him, and his camels were more abundant than before. Thereafter, he came to the Prophet and informed him of it, so the Prophet climbed the pulpit. He glorified Allah and praised Him and commanded the people to ask Allah and incline towards Him. Then he recited,

﴿وَمَن يَتَّقِ اللَّهَ يَجْعَل لَّهُ مَخْرَجًا ۝٢ وَيَرْزُقْهُ مِنْ حَيْثُ لَا يَحْتَسِبُ ۝٣﴾

Whoever fears Allah, He will give him a way out and provide for him from where he does not expect. (65:2–3)

1 *Mudd* and *ṣāʿ* are measurements of volume.

A man asked Thābit al-Bunānī to intercede on his behalf with a judge regarding a need he had. Thābit stood up with him, and whenever he passed by a masjid on the way he would enter and pray and supplicate there. He only arrived at the judge's council once he had left, so the one with the need reprimanded him because of that. He replied, 'I was only tending to your need.' Thereafter, Allah ﷻ fulfilled his need without needing to see the judge.

Isḥāq ibn ʿAbbād al-Baṣrī was asleep when he saw in his dream someone saying to him, 'Help the troubled one.' He awoke and asked if there was any needy person among his neighbours. They said, 'We do not know.' He then slept and he came a second and third time, saying, 'Are you sleeping when you have not yet helped the troubled one?' He got up and took three hundred dirhams with him. He mounted his mule and left for Basrah until he stopped at the door of the masjid where funeral prayers were being offered. He entered the masjid and there was a man praying. When he noticed him, he moved closer to him and said, 'Slave of Allah! At this hour? In this place? What is your need?' He replied, 'I had a capital of a hundred dirhams, but I lost it and was forced to take a debt of two hundred dirhams.' Isḥāq took out the dirhams and said, 'This is three hundred dirhams. Take it!' He took them, and then Isḥāq said, 'Do you recognise me?' He responded, 'No.' He said, 'I am Isḥāq ibn ʿAbbād. If you are ever afflicted with a calamity, come to me. I live in such-and-such place.' He told him, 'May Allah have mercy on you, but if a calamity were to befall us, we will take refuge with the One who brought you out at this hour to us.'

ʿAbd ar-Raḥmān ibn Zayd ibn Aslam said,

> One morning, my mother said to my father, 'By Allah, there is nothing in this house that a living thing can eat.' So he stood up, performed ablution, put on his clothes and then prayed in his home. Then my mother turned to me and said, 'Your father does nothing more than what you see. So you go out [to find food].' So I set out, and the thought of a friend of ours who sold dates crossed my mind, so I

> went to his shop to see him. When he saw me, he called out to me and took me to his home and fed me. He then took out a bag with thirty dinars for me, from himself, without me mentioning a thing about our situation and he said, 'Pass greetings on to your father and tell him that we have kept a portion of everything for him in our shop, and this is his share.'

Shaqīq al-Balkhī is reported to have said,

> I was sitting in my house when my wife said to me, 'Look at the hunger of these children! It is not lawful for you to make them carry a burden they cannot bear.' So I performed ablution. Then, the thought of a friend crossed my mind; he used to make me swear that I would inform him if I ever had a need and that I would not conceal it from him. So I left the house to go see him, but, passing by the masjid, I remembered a narration from Abū Jaʿfar: 'Whoever has a need with creation should first take it to Allah ﷻ.' Thus, I entered the masjid and offered two units of prayer. When I was in the sitting position, sleep overcame me. I saw in my dream some saying to me, 'Shaqīq! You turn the slaves to Allah but you yourself forget Him!' I awoke and realised that it was a warning that my Lord brought to my attention, so I stayed in the masjid until I had read the *'Ishā'* prayer. When I went home, I found the one whom I had intended to visit. Allah ﷻ motivated his heart; and by his hand, Allah ﷻ bestowed my family with what they needed.

It is related that Ibrāhīm ibn Adham left to go on an expedition with his companions. They agreed to share the expenses, each placed a dinar in the pot. [Ibrāhīm did not have a dinar,] so he pondered about which of his brothers he should ask for a loan; but then he came to his senses and wept, saying, 'Oh how shameful! I seek from the slaves, leaving their Lord, who says, "Who is more rightful of being asked? Me or My slaves?"' So he performed ablution, prayed and fell into prostration, saying,

> My Lord! You know what I have done! It was a mistake bourne out

> of my ignorance. If You punish me because of it, then I deserve it; and if You pardon me, then You have the right to. You know of my need, so fulfil it by Your mercy.

He then lifted his head and there, before him, was approximately four hundred dinars. He took one dinar from it and went on his way.

It is related that Aṣbagh ibn Zayd said,

> Once, me and my family had nothing to eat for three days. My younger daughter came out to me and said, 'Father! I am hungry.' So I came to the basin, performed ablution and offered two units of prayer. I was inspired with a supplication, at the end of which I begged, 'O Allah! Grant me sustenance from You. Do not give anyone the opportunity to have a favour over me and do not hold me responsible for it in the Hereafter. By Your mercy, O Most Merciful of those who show mercy.' I then returned home and my eldest daughter stood to meet me and said, 'Father! My uncle came a while ago with this bag of dirhams, a porter carrying flour and another carrying different products from the market and he said, "Pass greetings to my brother and tell him that if he ever needs anything to supplicate with this prayer and his need will be fulfilled."'

Aṣbagh said, 'By Allah! I have never had a brother and I do not know the one who said this, but Allah has power over all things!'

Ḥakam ibn Mūsā is reported to have said,

> One morning, my wife said to me, 'We have no flour, nor bread,' so I went out with no ability to do anything and ssupplicated in the street, 'O Allah! You know that I know that You know that I have no flour nor bread and no dirhams, so bring us that.' A man then met me and said, 'Do you want bread or flour?' I told him, 'Either of them.' Then I walked on for the whole day trying, but I had no ability to do anything. So I returned home and my wife brought out an abundance of bread and meat. I asked, 'Where did you get this?' She said, 'The One you turned to,' and I was speechless.

Awzāʿī said,

> I saw a man in *ṭawāf*, holding on to the drapes of the *Kaʿbah*, saying, 'O my Lord! I am needy, as You can see. My children have gone mad, as You can see; and my camel has become weak, as You can see. What do You see, O One who sees but is not seen?' Suddenly, someone called out behind him, "ʿĀṣim! ʿĀṣim! Go to your uncle! He has passed away in Ṭā'if and has left behind 1000 sheep, 300 camels, 400 dinars, four slaves and three Yemeni swords. Go and claim them for he has no other heir besides you.' I said, "ʿĀṣim! The One you called on is close to you.' So he said, 'O so-and-so! Have you not heard His words,
>
> ﴿وَإِذَا سَأَلَكَ عِبَادِى عَنِّى فَإِنِّى قَرِيبٌ﴾
>
> *If My slaves ask you about Me, I am near* (2:186)?'

Stories and narrations of this kind are numerous and mentioning them would prove lengthy, but they can be found in books such as *al-Faraj baʿd ash-Shiddah* and *Mujābī ad-Daʿwah* by Ibn Abī 'd-Dunyā, *al-Mustaṣrikhīn bi'llāh ʿinda Nuzūl al-Balā'* by Qāḍī Abū 'l-Walīd ibn aṣ-Ṣaffār and *al-Mustaghīthīn bi'llāh ʿinda Nuzūl al-Balā'* by Ḥāfiẓ Abū 'l-Qāsim ibn Bashkwāl al-Andalūsī and other books of asceticism, books of narrations that soften the heart and biographies of scholars.

Shaykh Abū 'l-Faraj relates in *at-Tārīkh al-Kabīr*, with a chain of narration from Ḥasan ibn Sufyān al-Fasawī,[1] that he was staying in Egypt with a group of his companions, writing hadith, when they became impoverished. They sold whatever they had until nothing remained for them to sell. They stayed hungry for three days, not finding anything to eat, and on the fourth day they decided to ask because of their desperate need. They cast lots to decide who from them would ask and the lot fell on Ḥasan ibn Sufyān, who says,

> I was bewildered and startled and my self did not allow me to ask. I

1 I have not come across a scholar by this name. There is, however, a narrator who is quoted in the books of hadith by the name of Ḥasan ibn Sufyān an-Nasawī, the teacher of Ibn Ḥibbān. He passed away in the year 915 CE. See Dhahabī, *Tārīkh al-Islām*, 7:66.

> diverted to a prayer room in the masjid, prayed two long units and supplicated to Allah ﷻ to remove the calamity and bring deliverance. I had not yet finished the prayer when a man entered the masjid with a slave who had a handkerchief in his hand. He said, 'Which one of you is Ḥasan ibn Sufyān?' I lifted my head from prostration and said, 'I am.' He then said that the Amīr Ibn Ṭūlūn extends his greetings and salutations to you, and apologises for his heedlessness in tending to your situation and his failure to uphold your rights. He has sent you what should suffice as expenditure for the time being. He is going to visit you tomorrow to apologise to you personally.' He placed in front of each of us a bag of a hundred dinars. We were amazed by this, so we asked why he was there. He said that, while he was sleeping, he saw a rider in the air, saying to him, 'Get up and go to Ḥasan ibn Sufyān and his companions. They have been hungry for three days in such-and-such masjid.' He asked the rider, 'Who are you?' and he replied, 'I am Riḍwān, the gatekeeper of Paradise.'

Ḥasan said, 'So we thanked Allah ﷻ and tended to our business. We left Egypt swiftly that night fearing that the Amīr would visit us and then people would come to know of our secret, propelling us into recognition and aclamation which would surely lead to ostentation and fame.'

The aforementioned is also related with a chain of narration from Muḥammad ibn Hārūn ar-Rūyānī that he was with Muḥammad ibn Naṣr al-Marwazī, Muḥammad ibn ʿAlawiyyah al-Warrāq and Muḥammad ibn Isḥāq ibn Khuzaymah; and he mentioned a similar story wherein the person who prayed and supplicated was Ibn Khuzaymah. Yet another chain of narration is mentioned wherein the four were Muḥammad ibn Jarīr, Muḥammad ibn Naṣr, Muḥammad ibn Khuzaymah and Muḥammad ibn Hārūn.

CHAPTER 6

When You Seek Assistance, Seek it from Allah ﷻ

After he ﷺ commanded us to be mindful of Allah ﷻ and to become acquainted with Him in times of ease—which is true worship—he ﷺ advised us to ask Allah ﷻ and supplicate to Him alone, since supplication *is* worship, as is mentioned in the hadith of Nuʿmān ibn Bashīr ﵁, quoted by the authors of the four *Sunans*. The Prophet ﷺ thereafter recited,

﴿وَقَالَ رَبُّكُمُ ادْعُونِي أَسْتَجِبْ لَكُمْ﴾

Your Lord says, 'Call on Me and I will answer you. (40:60)

Then he ﷺ advised [us] to seek assistance from Allah ﷻ alone. This is derived from His words,

﴿إِيَّاكَ نَعْبُدُ وَإِيَّاكَ نَسْتَعِينُ﴾

You alone we worship. You alone we ask for help. (1:5)

It is truly a sublime and extensive phrase, said to be the secret of all of the Divine Books and their foundation.

[HE ﷻ WILL ASSIST YOU IN RELIGIOUS AND WORLDLY INTERESTS]

Seeking the assistance Allah ﷻ alone has two benefits: the first is that the slave of Allah ﷻ cannot rely on himself in order to perform worship. The second is that he has no one to help him in his religious and worldly interests except Allah ﷻ. The one whom Allah ﷻ helps is the one who will be relieved and the one whom Allah ﷻ forsakes is the one who is deserted.

It is related from the Prophet ﷺ in the authentic hadith,

إِحْرِصْ عَلَى مَا يَنْفَعُكَ، وَاسْتَعِنْ بِاللهِ وَلَا تَعْجَزْ.

> Strive for what benefits you, seek assistance from Allah and do not lose heart.[1]

He ﷺ would say in his sermon and would teach his Companions ﷺ to say,

اَلْحَمْدُ لِلّٰهِ نَسْتَعِينُهُ وَنَسْتَهْدِيهِ.

> All praise is for Allah. We seek his assistance and ask Him for guidance.[2]

He ﷺ also commanded Muʿādh ibn Jabal ﷺ to not forget to say after every prayer,

اللّٰهُمَّ أَعِنِّي عَلَى ذِكْرِكَ وَشُكْرِكَ وَحُسْنِ عِبَادَتِك.

> O Allah! Help me to remember You, to thank You and worship You in a good manner.[3]

One of his supplications ﷺ was,

رَبِّ أَعِنِّي وَلا تُعِنْ عَلَيَّ.

---

1 Muslim (2664).

2 I have not found this hadith without the phrase *nastaghfiruhu*. Shāfiʿī mentions the hadith with *nastaghfiruhu* in his *Musnad*, p.67.

3 Abū Dāwūd (1522).

My Lord, help me and do not help anyone against me.[1]

It is narrated that the supplication of *qunūt* that ʿUmar and others ﷺ used to make included the following:

اللّٰهُمَّ إِنَّا نَسْتَعِينُكَ وَنَسْتَهْدِيكَ.

O Allah! We seek Your assistance and we ask You for guidance.[2]

The following is mentioned in a famous narration, and Mūsā ﷺ is reported to have said it when he struck the sea, causing it to split:

اللّٰهُمَّ لَكَ الْحَمْدُ، وَإِلَيْكَ الْمُشْتَكَى، وَأَنْتَ الْمُسْتَعَانُ، وَبِكَ الْمُسْتَغَاثُ، وَعَلَيْكَ التُّكْلَانُ، وَلَا حَوْلَ وَلَا قُوَّةَ إِلَّا بِاللّٰهِ.

O Allah! All praise is for You and to You are brought grievances. You are the Help, relief is with You and all reliance is on You. There is no power and no might except with You.[3]

These supplications show that the slave of Allah ﷻ needs His assistance in carrying out obligations, staying away from prohibitions and patiently bearing fate, as Yaʿqūb ﷺ said to his sons,

﴿فَصَبْرٌ جَمِيلٌ وَاللّٰهُ الْمُسْتَعَانُ عَلَىٰ مَا تَصِفُونَ﴾

But beauty lies in showing patience. It is Allah alone who is my Help. (12:18)

This is why ʿĀ'ishah ﷺ said this phrase when the people of the Slander accused her, and Allah ﷻ subsequently declared her innocent of their charge.[4]

Mūsā ﷺ said to his people,

﴿اسْتَعِينُوا بِاللّٰهِ وَاصْبِرُوا﴾

1 Aḥmad (1997).

2 ʿAbd ar-Razzāq quotes this supplication from ʿAlī ﷺ (4978).

3 Bayhaqī, *ad-Daʿawāt al-Kabīr* (264); Ṭabarānī, *Awsaṭ* (3394) have quoted variations of this supplication.

4 Bukhārī (2661); Muslim (2770).

Seek help in Allah and be patient. (7:128)

And Allah ﷻ said to His Prophet Muhammad ﷺ,

﴿قَالَ رَبِّ احْكُمْ بِالْحَقِّ وَرَبُّنَا الرَّحْمَٰنُ الْمُسْتَعَانُ عَلَىٰ مَا تَصِفُونَ﴾

Say: 'Lord, judge with truth! Our Lord is the All-Merciful, the One whose help is sought.' (21:112)

When he ﷺ gave ʿUthmān ؓ glad tidings of Paradise for the calamities that will befall him, he said, 'Allah is the One Whose help is sought.' When the rebels entered upon ʿUthmān ؓ and struck him, he said, while blood flowed from him, 'There is no god but You! Glory be to You! Indeed, I have been one of the wrongdoers. O Allah! I seek Your assistance against them and seek Your assistance in all my matters. I ask You for patience in the test You have given me.'

Abū 'sh-Shaykh al-Iṣbahānī quoted from Abū Ṭalḥah ؓ that when the Prophet ﷺ met the enemy in one of his battles, he said,

يَا مَالِكَ يَوْمِ الدِّينِ، إِيَّاكَ نَعْبُدُ وَإِيَّاكَ نَسْتَعِينُ.

'O King of the Day of the Repayment. You alone we worship. You alone we ask for help.'[1] Abū Ṭalḥah ؓ said, '[As a result of that,] I saw men dropping to the ground.'

So the slave is in need of Allah's ﷻ assistance in his religious and worldly interests, as Zubayr ؓ explained to his son, ʿAbdullāh, advising him to settle his debts: 'If you unable to, then seek help from my Master.' So he asked him, 'Beloved father! Who is your master?' He said, 'Allah.' ʿAbdullāh asked, 'Whenever I fell into any difficulty in settling my father's debt, I said, "O Master of Zubayr! Settle his debt," and He would settle it.'[2]

ʿUmar ibn al-Khaṭṭāb ؓ said in the first sermon he delivered on the pulpit, 'Know that the Arabs are like a proud camel whose halter

1 Ibn as-Sunnī (334).
2 Bukhārī (3129).

I have taken. I will take it to its destination, seeking Allah's help in doing so.'

[HE ﷻ WILL ASSIST YOU IN DEATH AND BEYOND]

Likewise, the slave is in need of Allah's ﷻ assistance in the terrors of death and beyond that face him. When death approached Khālid ibn Walīd ﵁, a man from those around him said, 'By Allah, he does not like death.' Khālid ﵁ said, 'Of course! Which is why I ask Allah ﷻ for His assistance.'

ʿĀmir ibn ʿAbdillāh ibn az-Zubayr wept at the time of his death and said, 'I am only weeping for the heat of the day and the cold of standing,' meaning fasting during the day and standing in prayer during the night. He said, 'And I am here, before Allah ﷻ, asking His help with this death of mine.'

One of the early Muslims said, 'O my Lord! I am amazed at how the one who recognises You can hope for someone other than You. I am amazed at how the one who recognises You can ask anyone other than You for help!'

Ḥasan wrote to ʿUmar ibn ʿAbd al-ʿAzīz, 'Do not seek help from anyone other than Allah ﷻ lest Allah hand you over to him.'

One of the scholars said, 'Be satisfied with Allah ﷻ and seek His assistance, for He is indeed the best whose help is sought.'

CHAPTER 7

The Pens Have Dried Regarding What is to Be

In another narration, there is: 'The pens have been lifted and the books have dried.'[1] And in yet another narration: 'The pages have dried.'[2]

All of these are metaphors for the influence of fate and its complete inscription in a comprehensive book aeons ago. When a book has been written and completed and time has passed over it, the pens used to write it are lifted and their ink dries up, and the pages which were written also dry up. This is the best metaphor and the most eloquent one. The Book of Allah ﷻ and the Sunnah have indicated this same meaning.

Allah ﷻ says,

﴿مَا أَصَابَ مِنْ مُصِيبَةٍ فِي الْأَرْضِ وَلَا فِي أَنْفُسِكُمْ إِلَّا فِي كِتَابٍ مِنْ قَبْلِ أَنْ نَبْرَأَهَا إِنَّ ذَلِكَ عَلَى اللهِ يَسِيرٌ﴾

Nothing occurs, either in the earth or in yourselves, without its being in a book before We make it happen. That is something easy for Allah. (57:22)

Ḍaḥḥāk said, relating from Ibn ʿAbbās ﵄,

Indeed, Allah ﷻ created the Pen and commanded it to write with His

1 Aḥmad (2763).

2 Tirmidhī (2516).

> permission. The scale of the Pen is as vast as the breadth of the heavens and the earth. The Pen asked, 'What should I write, my Lord?' He said, 'My creation, which I am going to create and establish, such as the rain, plants, souls, impressions—meaning deeds—sustenance and appointed times.' Thus, the Pen wrote all that is to be until the Day of Rising and Allah ratified it in the written book which is with Him under the Throne.

Abū Ẓabyān related that Ibn ʿAbbās said, 'The first thing that Allah created was the Pen. Then He said to it, "Write!" It said, "What shall I write?" Allah said, "Fate." So it wrote what is to be until the Hour arrives.' He then recited,

﴿ن وَالْقَلَمِ وَمَا يَسْطُرُونَ﴾

Nūn. By the Pen and what they write down! (68:1)

Abū Ḍuḥā relates something similar from Ibn ʿAbbās. This hadith is also related to the Prophet himself, but its ascription to him cannot be established.

Ibn Baṭṭah, with a weak chain of narration, related from Abū Hurayrah who relates from the Prophet,

> The first thing Allah created was the Pen. Then He created Nūn, which is the inkwell. He then said, 'Write!' It said, 'What shall I write?' He said, 'Write what is going to be until the Day of Rising.' That is the meaning of His words: *Nūn. By the Pen and what they write down!* Then He sealed the Pen and it did not speak, and it will not speak until the Day of Rising.[1]

Imam Aḥmad, Abū Dāwūd and Tirmidhī quoted the hadith of ʿUbādah ibn aṣ-Ṣāmit that the Prophet said,

إِنَّ أَوَّلَ مَا خَلَقَ اللهُ الْقَلَمُ، ثُمَّ قَالَ: اكْتُبْ! فَجَرَى فِي تِلْكَ السَّاعَةِ بِمَا هُوَ كَائِنٌ إِلَى يَوْمِ الْقِيَامَةِ.

1 Ibn Kathīr quotes a variation of this hadith (8:185).

The first thing that Allah ﷻ created was the Pen. Then He said to it, 'Write!' At that moment, it wrote what is going to be until the Day of Rising.[1]

In the *Ṣaḥīḥ* of Muslim there is the narration of ʿAbdullāh ibn ʿAmr ؓ that the Prophet ﷺ said,

إِنَّ اللهَ كَتَبَ مَقَادِيرَ الْخَلَائِقِ قَبْلَ أَنْ يَخْلُقَ السَّمَاوَاتِ وَالْأَرْضَ بِخَمْسِينَ أَلْفَ سَنَةٍ.

Indeed, Allah ﷻ wrote the fates of creation fifty thousand years before He created the heavens and the earth.[2]

Imam Aḥmad, Tirmidhī and Nasāʾī quote the hadith of ʿAbdullāh ibn ʿAmr ؓ who said,

خَرَجَ عَلَيْنَا رَسُولُ اللهِ ﷺ وَفِي يَدِهِ كِتَابَانِ، فَقَالَ: أَتَدْرُونَ مَا هَذَانِ الْكِتَابَانِ؟ فَقُلْنَا: لَا يَا رَسُولَ اللهِ إِلَّا أَنْ تُخْبِرَنَا. فَقَالَ لِلَّذِي فِي يَدِهِ الْيُمْنَى: هَذَا كِتَابٌ مِنْ رَبِّ الْعَالَمِينَ فِيهِ أَسْمَاءُ أَهْلِ الْجَنَّةِ وَأَسْمَاءُ آبَائِهِمْ وَقَبَائِلِهِمْ، ثُمَّ أُجْمِلَ عَلَى آخِرِهِمْ فَلَا يُزَادُ فِيهِمْ وَلَا يُنْقَصُ مِنْهُمْ أَبَدًا. ثُمَّ قَالَ لِلَّذِي فِي شِمَالِهِ: هَذَا كِتَابٌ مِنْ رَبِّ الْعَالَمِينَ فِيهِ أَسْمَاءُ أَهْلِ النَّارِ وَأَسْمَاءُ آبَائِهِمْ وَقَبَائِلِهِمْ، ثُمَّ أُجْمِلَ عَلَى آخِرِهِمْ فَلَا يُزَادُ فِيهِمْ وَلَا يُنْقَصُ مِنْهُمْ أَبَدًا. فَقَالَ أَصْحَابُهُ: فَفِيمَ الْعَمَلُ يَا رَسُولَ اللهِ إِنْ كَانَ أَمْرٌ قَدْ فُرِغَ مِنْهُ؟ فَقَالَ: سَدِّدُوا وَقَارِبُوا، فَإِنَّ صَاحِبَ الْجَنَّةِ يُخْتَمُ لَهُ بِعَمَلِ أَهْلِ الْجَنَّةِ وَإِنْ عَمِلَ أَيَّ عَمَلٍ، وَإِنَّ صَاحِبَ النَّارِ يُخْتَمُ لَهُ بِعَمَلِ أَهْلِ النَّارِ وَإِنْ عَمِلَ أَيَّ عَمَلٍ. ثُمَّ قَالَ رَسُولُ اللهِ ﷺ بِيَدَيْهِ فَنَبَذَهُمَا، ثُمَّ قَالَ: فَرَغَ رَبُّكُمْ مِنَ الْعِبَادِ فَرِيقٌ فِي الْجَنَّةِ وَفَرِيقٌ فِي السَّعِيرِ.

One day, the Messenger of Allah ﷺ appeared before us with two books in his hands and said, 'Do you know what these two books are?' We

1 Aḥmad (22705); Abū Dāwūd (4700); Tirmidhī (3319).

2 Muslim (2653).

said, 'Not unless you tell us, Messenger of Allah!' He ﷺ said about the one in his right hand, 'This is a book from the Lord of all the worlds which contains the names of the people of Paradise, their fathers' names and their tribes. They are all included, up to the last man. There will never be an increase in them nor a decrease from them.' Then he ﷺ said about the one in his left hand, 'This is a book from the Lord of all the worlds which contains the names of the inmates of the Fire, their fathers' names and their tribes. They are all included, up to the last man. There will never be an increase in them nor a decrease from them.' His Companions ؓ asked, 'Messenger of Allah! Then what is the point of deeds if the matter has been decided?' He ﷺ said, 'Seek what is balanced and correct and draw near, for the fate of the people of Paradise is sealed with deeds of the people of Paradise, regardless of any other deeds they have done. And the fate of the inmates of the Fire is sealed with the deeds of the inmates of the Fire, regardless of any other deeds they have done.' Then the Messenger of Allah ﷺ gestured with his hands, casting them aside and said, 'Your Lord is done with His slaves; a group will be in Paradise and a group in the Fire.'[1]

Imam Aḥmad quotes the hadith of Abū 'd-Dardā' ؓ from the Prophet ﷺ,

فَرَغَ اللهُ إِلَى كُلِّ عَبْدٍ مِنْ خَمْسٍ: مِنْ أَجَلِهِ وَرِزْقِهِ وَأَثَرِهِ وَشَقِيٌّ أَمْ سَعِيدٍ.

Allah has concluded five for every slave: his death, his provisions, his deeds and whether he is wretched or fortunate.[2]

Imam Aḥmad and Tirmidhī quote the hadith of Ibn Masʿūd ؓ that the Prophet ﷺ said,

خَلَقَ اللهُ كُلَّ نَفْسٍ وَكَتَبَ حَيَاتَهَا وَرِزْقَهَا وَمَصَائِبَهَا.

Allah ﷻ created every soul and wrote their lives, their provisions and their tribulations.[3]

---

1 Aḥmad (6563); Tirmidhī (2141).

2 Aḥmad (21723).

3 Aḥmad (4198); Tirmidhī (2143).

Muslim quotes from the hadith of Jābir ﷺ that a man said,

يَا رَسُوْلَ اللهِ فِيمَا الْعَمَلُ الْيَوْمَ؟ أَفِيمَا جَفَّتْ بِهِ الْأَقْلَامُ، وَجَرَتْ بِهِ الْمَقَادِيرُ، أَمْ فِيمَا نَسْتَقْبِلُ؟ قَالَ: لَا، بَلْ فِيمَا جَفَّتْ بِهِ الْأَقْلَامُ وَجَرَتْ بِهِ الْمَقَادِيرُ. قَالَ: فَفِيمَ الْعَمَلُ؟ فَقَالَ: اعْمَلُوا فَكُلٌّ مُيَسَّرٌ.

> Messenger of Allah! What of the deeds of today? Are they because the pens have dried and the divine decree is decided, or are they for our future?' He ﷺ said, 'Rather, they are because the pens have dried and the divine decree is decided.' They asked, 'Then what is the point of deeds?' To which he ﷺ replied, 'Do good deeds, for everyone is facilitated [towards his fate].[1]

There are numerous hadiths with this meaning and likewise many narrations from the Companions ﷺ. One of the scholars said,

> Surrender the whole matter, for the Pen of existence has dried. Humankind has a Creator and there is no rebelling against His decision.

1 Muslim (2648).

CHAPTER 8

On Benefit and Harm Being Ordained

[The hadith that is the topic of this book continues,][1]

> If all of creation together wanted to benefit you with something that Allah has not destined, they would not be able to do it. And if they wanted to harm you with something that Allah has not ordained against you, they would not be able to do it.

What he ﷺ means by the aforementioned is that whatever happens to the slave of Allah ﷻ in his worldly matters, whether harm or benefit, it is all destined for him. And something that is not written for him and not destined for him can never happen to him, even if all of creation together tried to make it happen. The Qur'an has also indicated this similar meaning in His ﷻ words,

﴿قُلْ لَنْ يُصِيبَنَا إِلَّا مَا كَتَبَ اللَّهُ لَنَا﴾

> *Say: 'Nothing can happen to us except what Allah has ordained for us.'* (9:51)

In addition, His ﷻ words,

1 The above is an amended chapter heading. The chapter of the Arabic original is the part of the hadith which is quoted at the beginning of the chapter.

﴿مَا أَصَابَ مِنْ مُصِيبَةٍ فِي الْأَرْضِ وَلَا فِي أَنْفُسِكُمْ إِلَّا فِي كِتَابٍ﴾

Nothing occurs, either in the earth or in yourselves, without its being in a book. (57:22)

In addition, His ﷻ words,

﴿قُلْ لَوْ كُنْتُمْ فِي بُيُوتِكُمْ لَبَرَزَ الَّذِينَ كُتِبَ عَلَيْهِمُ الْقَتْلُ إِلَى مَضَاجِعِهِمْ﴾

Say: 'Even if you had been inside your homes, those people for whom being killed was decreed would have gone out to their place of death.' (3:154)

Imam Aḥmad quotes the hadith of Abū 'd-Dardā' ؓ that the Prophet ﷺ said,

إِنَّ لِكُلِّ شَيْءٍ حَقِيقَةً، وَمَا بَلَغَ عَبْدٌ حَقِيقَةَ الْإِيمَانِ حَتَّى يَعْلَمَ أَنَّ مَا أَصَابَهُ لَمْ يَكُنْ لِيُخْطِئَهُ، وَمَا أَخْطَأَهُ لَمْ يَكُنْ لِيُصِيبَهُ.

Everything has a reality, and a slave of Allah can never achieve the reality of faith until he knows that what afflicted him was never going to miss him, and that what missed him was never going to afflict him.[1]

Abū Dāwūd and Ibn Mājah too quote the hadith of Zayd ibn Thābit ؓ from the Prophet ﷺ with this meaning.[2]

[PRINCIPAL MESSAGE OF THIS HADITH]

The whole of the Prophet's ﷺ advice to Ibn ʿAbbās ؓ revolves around this core concept, and what follows it and precedes it are branches of it, and they depend on it. Therefore, if the slave knows that no good or bad and benefit or harm can affect him except for what Allah ﷻ has written for him, and that the whole of creation together trying to do contrary to what is destined will have absolutely no benefit, then he will know that Allah ﷻ alone is the One who harms, the One who benefits, the Bestower and the Preventer. Once he knows that, then

1 Aḥmad (27490).
2 Abū Dāwūd (4699); Ibn Mājah (77).

the slave of Allah ﷻ must declare his Lord ﷻ alone as the One whose assistance is sought, the One who is asked, implored and supplicated to. He must also worship and obey only Him ﷻ, since the purpose of worshipping one who is worshipped is to gain benefit and repel harm. This is why Allah ﷻ rebukes one who worships what cannot benefit or harm nor does it avail the worshipper in any way. There are many who do not have belief established in their hearts, and they prefer obedience to creation over obedience to Allah ﷻ, hoping they will benefit them or repel harm from them. Yet, if the slave establishes that Allah ﷻ alone benefits, harms, grants and repels, then that must lead him to obey and worship Him alone, and he will prefer His obedience over the obedience of all of creation. This understanding, that Allah alone harms and benefits, must also lead to the realisation that Allah ﷻ alone should be asked and only His assistance should be sought.

This exhaustive, amazing counsel contains all of these pertinent points. If a slave of Allah ﷻ is mindful of Him, then he is mindful of His limits and upholding His rights (the essence of worshipping Him)—which was the first point introduced in this counsel. The consequence of that is that Allah ﷻ is mindful of His slave, which is ultimately what the slave seeks from his Lord ﷻ. That is then followed by becoming acquainted with Allah ﷻ in times of ease, as it is a requirement for Allah ﷻ recognising His slave in times of difficulty, which is the perfection of Allah's recognition of His slave and is included in it.

In the counsel, only times of difficulty are mentioned: 'He will recognise you in times of hardship' since this is when the slave desperately needs someone to acknowledge him and save him. In this state, even those who associate partners with Allah ﷻ are sincere in their supplication to Allah ﷻ alone. They ask and seek only from Him because they know that none can remove harm except Him ﷻ. Then when the harm is removed, they start associating partners with Him again, as He has mentioned about them and censured them in various places in His Book.[1] He ﷻ commanded us to oppose them

1 Qur'an 10:22–23 and 29:65.

and contradict their habits by becoming acquainted with Allah ﷻ in times of ease with sincerity for His Religion, by obeying Him and seeking His proximity. The consequence of this is Allah ﷻ recognises us in times of hardship and help us navigate our way out of them.

The Prophet ﷺ then followed that by encouraging asking Allah ﷻ alone and seeking only His assistance, both in times of difficulty and ease. Thereafter, he ﷺ mentioned the comprehensive principle upon which these issues are based: recognising that Allah ﷻ alone bestows benefit, inflicts harm, grants goodness and repels evil. None of these can affect the slave of Allah ﷻ unless He has destined and preordained it for him; in fact, the whole of creation combined is incapable of bestowing benefit or inflicting harm which is not destined in the Preordained Book.

[SEVERING TIES WITH CREATION]

This can only be realised when the slave of Allah ﷻ severs ties with creation: from asking them, seeking assistance from them, hoping that they will bestow benefit or remove harm and fearing that they will inflict harm or prevent benefit. This too demands that Allah ﷻ alone be obeyed and worshipped, that His obedience be preferred over the obedience of the whole of creation and that His displeasure be feared even though that means the displeasure of the whole of creation. It has be narrated in the hadith of Abū Saʿīd ﵁ that the Prophet ﷺ said,

إِنَّ مِنْ ضَعْفِ الْيَقِينِ أَنْ تُرْضِيَ النَّاسَ بِسَخَطِ اللهِ، وَأَنْ تَحْمَدَهُمْ عَلَى رِزْقِ اللهِ، وَأَنْ تَذُمَّهُمْ عَلَى مَا لَمْ يُؤْتِكَ اللهُ، إِنَّ رِزْقَ اللهِ لَا يَجُرُّهُ حِرْصُ حَرِيصٍ، وَلَا يَرُدُّهُ كَرَاهَةُ كَارِهٍ.

> Symptoms of uncertainty are that you please people at the cost of Allah's pleasure, that you praise them for Allah's provisions and that you find fault with them for something Allah ﷻ did not give

you. The desire of the covetous cannot find the provision of Allah for you and the hate of the averse cannot repel it from you.[1]

How excellent is the [following] statement of one the predecessors!

If only you were delighted, though life is bitter!
And if only you were pleased, though creation is angry!
If only there was prosperity between me and You,
And between me and the worlds only desolation.
If love from you was true, everything would be insignificant,
And everyone on the earth would be just earth.

When an individual realises that all of creation on earth are made of the same substance: soil, then how could he prefer obedience to some soil over obedience to the Lord of lords ﷻ? Or how can the pleasure of soil be sought at the cost of the pleasure of the Ever-Giving King? This truly is a strange thing! The Qur'an has pointed to this principle of recognising that bestowing and preventing is only in Allah's Hands, in numerous places, such as His words,

﴿مَا يَفْتَحِ اللهُ لِلنَّاسِ مِنْ رَحْمَةٍ فَلَا مُمْسِكَ لَهَا وَمَا يُمْسِكْ فَلَا مُرْسِلَ لَهُ مِنْ بَعْدِهِ﴾

Any mercy Allah opens up to people, no one can withhold; and any He withholds, no one can afterwards release. (35:2)

Also the words of Allah ﷻ,

﴿وَإِنْ يَمْسَسْكَ اللهُ بِضُرٍّ فَلَا كَاشِفَ لَهُ إِلَّا هُوَ وَإِنْ يُرِدْكَ بِخَيْرٍ فَلَا رَادَّ لِفَضْلِهِ﴾

If Allah afflicts you with harm, no one can remove it except Him. If He desires good for you, no one can avert His favour. (10:107)

Then there are His ﷻ words,

---

1 Bayhaqī, *Shuʿab* (203).

﴿قُلْ أَفَرَأَيْتُم مَّا تَدْعُونَ مِن دُونِ اللَّهِ إِنْ أَرَادَنِيَ اللَّهُ بِضُرٍّ هَلْ هُنَّ كَاشِفَاتُ
ضُرِّهِ أَوْ أَرَادَنِي بِرَحْمَةٍ هَلْ هُنَّ مُمْسِكَاتُ رَحْمَتِهِ قُلْ حَسْبِيَ اللَّهُ عَلَيْهِ يَتَوَكَّلُ
الْمُتَوَكِّلُونَ﴾

Say: 'So what do you think? If Allah desires harm for me, can those you call upon besides Allah remove His harm? Or if He desires mercy for me, can they withhold His mercy?' Say: 'Allah is enough for me. All those who truly trust put their trust in Him.' (39:38)

In addition, there are His words relating what His prophet Nūḥ said to his people:

﴿يَاقَوْمِ إِن كَانَ كَبُرَ عَلَيْكُم مَّقَامِي وَتَذْكِيرِي بِآيَاتِ اللَّهِ فَعَلَى اللَّهِ تَوَكَّلْتُ
فَأَجْمِعُوا أَمْرَكُمْ وَشُرَكَاءَكُمْ﴾

My people, if my standing here and reminding you of Allah's Signs has become too much for you to bear, know that I have put my trust in Allah. So decide, you and your gods, on what you want to do. (10:71)

And there are His words, relating from His prophet Hūd,

﴿إِنِّي أُشْهِدُ اللَّهَ وَاشْهَدُوا أَنِّي بَرِيءٌ مِّمَّا تُشْرِكُونَ ﴿٥٤﴾ مِن دُونِهِ فَكِيدُونِي
جَمِيعًا ثُمَّ لَا تُنظِرُونِ ﴿٥٥﴾ إِنِّي تَوَكَّلْتُ عَلَى اللَّهِ رَبِّي وَرَبِّكُم ﴿٥٦﴾﴾

I call on Allah to be my witness, and you also bear witness, that I am free of all the gods you have apart from Him. So scheme against me, all of you together, and then grant me no respite. I have put my trust in Allah, my Lord and Your Lord. (11:54–56)

One of the early Muslims said,

What Allah has destined for me is sure to reach me.
    Who is there that can repel destiny with precaution?
Allah is more entitled to us than we are to ourselves.
    We are nothing but owned property.

A man complained to Fuḍayl about poverty, so Fuḍayl said to him, 'Do you seek a manager other than Allah?'

One of the early pious Muslims said,

Plan but the plan will avail you naught,
As fate will not pass you by with all your plans.
All matters have a Lord who manages them,
And whatever the Lord has determined, fate drives it forward.

CHAPTER 9

Know That Much Good Comes from Patience in the Face of What You Dislike

In the narration of ʿUmar, the freed slave of Ghafrah ibn ʿAbbās ﵄, there is an addition before these words, which says, 'Carry on doing deeds for Allah with certainty and satisfaction, if you can manage it, but if you are not able to do so, then indeed there is much good that comes from patience in the face of what you dislike.'[1]

The meaning of *yaqīn* (certainty) here is firm belief in predestined fate, as is mentioned explicitly in the narration Ibn ʿAbbās' ﵄ son, ʿAlī ibn ʿAbdillāh ibn ʿAbbās ﵄, who relates from him, albeit with a weak chain of narration. In it is the addition, 'I said, "Messenger of Allah! How should I deal with certainty?" He ﷺ said, "You should know that whatever befalls you was never going to pass you by and whatever passes you by was never going to befall you."'[2]

[SATISFACTION WITH FATE (RAḌĀʾ BIʾL-QAḌĀʾ)]

Opening the door of certainty[3] in preordained fate and determined destiny in the heart causes a person to feel satisfied with fate and

1 Bayhaqī, *al-Qaḍāʾ waʾl-Qadr* (306), (307).

2 Shajarī, *Tartīb al-Amālī* (2393).

3 Shajarī records this as part of the hadith, but in the copy of *Nūr al-Iqtibās* (p.109),

destiny, putting his heart at peace with it. The Qur'an has pointed to this specific meaning in His words,

﴿لِكَيْلَا تَأْسَوْا عَلَىٰ مَا فَاتَكُمْ وَلَا تَفْرَحُوا بِمَا آتَاكُمْ﴾

That is so that you will not be grieved about the things that pass you by or exult about the things that come to you. (57:23)

Ibn Abī 'd-Dunyā has quoted that Ḍaḥḥāk explained this verse,

> [It means,] console them so that you will not be grieved about the things that pass you by. Do not grieve about any matter of the world, since We have not destined it for you. Do not exult about anything that We have given to you from the world, since it was never going to be hidden from you.

Ibn Abī Ḥātim realted from Saʿīd ibn Jubayr that the verse means, 'So that you will not be grieved about wellbeing or abundance passing you by, since you know that that was written for you before He created you.'

One of the early Muslims said something with a similar meaning, 'Belief in fate removes grief and sorrow.'

The Prophet ﷺ indicated this meaning in the authentic narration from him,

احْرِصْ عَلَى مَا يَنْفَعُكَ، وَاسْتَعِنْ بِاللهِ وَلَا تَعْجَزْ، فَإِنْ أَصَابَكَ شَيْءٌ فَلَا تَقُلْ: لَوْ أَنِّي فَعَلْتُ كَذَا، وَلَكِنْ قُلْ: قَدَرُ اللهِ وَمَا شَاءَ فَعَلَ، فَإِنَّ لَوْ تَفْتَحُ عَمَلَ الشَّيْطَانِ.

> Desire what will benefit you, seek Allah's assistance and do not lose heart. If something befalls you do not say, "If only I did this and that." Rather, say, "Allah's divine decree and He does what He wills." Indeed, 'if only' opens a person up to Shayṭān's exploits.'[1]

it is written as part of Ibn Rajab's words. If it is part of the hadith, it will be translated as: 'Then you have opened the door of certainty.'

1 Muslim (2664).

This means that reminding oneself of preordained fate at times of difficulty removes the whispers of Shayṭān that cause grief, sorrow and regret, for pursuing the means to try and prevent it from happening.

Imam Aḥmad quotes the narration with the following addition, as reported by Anas ﵁,

خَدَمْتُ النَّبِيَّ ﷺ عَشْرَ سِنِينَ، فَمَا قَالَ لِي لِشَيْءٍ فَعَلْتُهُ: لَمَ فَعَلْتَ كَذَا وَكَذَا؟ وَلَا لِشَيْءٍ لَمْ أَفْعَلْهُ: أَلَا فَعَلْتَ كَذَا؟ وَكَانَ إِذَا لَامَنِي بَعْضُ أَهْلِهِ قَالَ: دَعْهُ فَلَوْ قُدِّرَ شَيْءٌ كَانَ.

> I served the Prophet ﷺ for ten years. Never did he say about a thing I did, 'Why did you do such-and-such?' Nor about a thing I did not do, 'Have you not done such-and-such?' If any of his family rebuked me, he ﷺ would say, 'Leave him. If something is destined it will be.'[1]

Ibn Abī 'd-Dunyā quotes a narration with a questionable chain of narration from ʿĀ'ishah ﵂: 'When the Prophet ﷺ was in his home, he would always say, "Whatever is destined will be."' He also quotes a narration (missing the Companion from the chain) that the Prophet ﷺ said to Ibn Masʿūd ﵁, 'Do not worry too much! Whatever is destined will be and whatever provisions you are allotted will come to you.'[2]

Ṭabarānī and Ḥākim have quoted the hadith of Abū Hurayrah ﵁ that the Prophet ﷺ said,

لَا حَوْلَ وَلَا قُوَّةَ إِلَّا بِاللهِ، دَوَاءٌ مِنْ تِسْعَةٍ وَتِسْعِينَ دَاءً أَيْسَرُهَا الْهَمُّ.

> 'There is no strength nor power except by Allah' is a cure for 99 illnesses, the lightest of which is grief.[3]

The realisation of this phrase demands entrusting all matters to Allah ﷻ. Nothing can be except what He wishes, and belief in that removes grief and sorrow. The Prophet ﷺ advised a man, saying,

1 Aḥmad (13418).
2 Ibn Abī 'd-Dunyā, *Faraj* (20).
3 Ṭabarānī, *Awsaṭ* (5028); Ḥākim (1990).

لَا تَتَّهِمِ اللهَ فِي شَيْءٍ قَضَاهُ لَكَ.

Do not question Allah in anything He has destined for you.[1]

If a believer sees that fate and destiny are from the wisdom and mercy of Allah ﷻ, and that He cannot be questioned in His decree, then that will lead him to being satisfied with the divine decree. Allah ﷻ says,

﴿مَا أَصَابَ مِنْ مُصِيبَةٍ إِلَّا بِإِذْنِ اللهِ وَمَنْ يُؤْمِنْ بِاللهِ يَهْدِ قَلْبَهُ﴾

No misfortune occurs except by Allah's permission. Whoever believes in Allah, He will guide his heart. (64:11)

ʿAlqamah said regarding this verse, 'It is a misfortune that befalls a person, but he knows that it is from Allah ﷻ, so he accepts it and is satisfied.'

The Prophet ﷺ said in an authentic hadith,

لَا يَقْضِي اللهُ لِلْمُؤْمِنِ قَضَاءً إِلَّا كَانَ خَيْرًا لَهُ، إِنْ أَصَابَتْهُ سَرَّاءُ شَكَرَ كَانَ خَيْرًا لَهُ، وَإِنْ أَصَابَتْهُ ضَرَّاءُ صَبَرَ كَانَ خَيْرًا لَهُ، وَلَيْسَ ذَلِكَ إِلَّا لِلْمُؤْمِنِ.

Allah ﷻ does not decree a matter for a believer except that it is good for him. If good comes to him, he is thankful and that is good for him. If hardship befalls him, he is patient and that is good for him. This is not the case with anyone except a believer.[2]

The Qur'an points to a similar meaning in His ﷻ words,

قُلْ لَنْ يُصِيبَنَا إِلَّا مَا كَتَبَ اللهُ لَنَا هُوَ مَوْلَانَا وَعَلَى اللهِ فَلْيَتَوَكَّلِ الْمُؤْمِنُونَ – قُلْ هَلْ تَرَبَّصُونَ بِنَا إِلَّا إِحْدَى الْحُسْنَيَيْنِ

Say: 'Nothing can happen to us except what Allah has ordained for us. He is our Master. It is in Allah that the believers should put their trust.' Say: 'What do you await for us except for one of the two best things?' (9:51–52)

He ﷻ says that nothing will afflict them except what He has ordained

1 Aḥmad (22717).
2 Muslim (2999).

for them, indicating that He ﷻ is all the same to them in every situation, whether it is favourable or not. He ﷻ informs them that He is their Master; and whoever takes Allah as a Master, He will not disgrace him. Rather, He will take responsibility of his affairs. Allah ﷻ says,

﴿فَاعْلَمُوا أَنَّ اللهَ مَوْلَاكُمْ نِعْمَ الْمَوْلَى وَنِعْمَ النَّصِيرُ﴾

> *Know that Allah is your Master, the Best Master and the Best of Helpers!* (8:40)

He ﷻ then followed that with His words,

﴿هَلْ تَرَبَّصُونَ بِنَا إِلَّا إِحْدَى الْحُسْنَيَيْنِ﴾

> *Say: 'What do you await for us except for one of the two best things?'* (9:51)

This means either victory and success or martyrdom. Whichever of the two it is, it is good.

Tirmidhī quotes the hadith of Anas ﷺ from the Prophet ﷺ,

إِنَّ اللهَ إِذَا أَحَبَّ قَوْمًا ابْتَلَاهُمْ، فَمَنْ رَضِيَ فَلَهُ الرِّضَا، وَمَنْ سَخِطَ فَلَهُ السَّخَطُ.

> When Allah loves a people, He afflicts them. Whoever is content with that will receive Allah's pleasure and whoever is discontent will receive Allah's resentment.[1]

Abū 'd-Dardā' ﷺ said, 'When Allah ﷻ decrees a matter, He loves for it to be accepted with pleasure.'

Umm ad-Dardā' ﷺ said, 'The ones who are content with Allah's decree are those who accept what He has decreed for them. In Paradise they will have houses which the martyrs will envy on the Day of Rising.'

Ibn Masʿūd ﷺ said, 'Allah ﷻ, in His justice and knowledge, has placed comfort and happiness in certainty and acceptance, and has placed grief and sorrow in doubt and resentment.' This has also been

1 Tirmidhī (2396).

related from the Prophet ﷺ, albeit with a weakness [in its chain of transmission].[1]

ʿUmar ibn ʿAbd al-ʿAzīz used to say, 'These invitations have left me and I have no desire in any matter except in places that Allah ﷻ has determined.' He often used to make this supplication, 'O Allah! Make me satisfied with Your divine decree and bless me in Your destiny, so that I do not want to hasten something You have delayed or delay something you have brought forward.'

Ibn ʿAwn said,

> Be content with the divine decree of Allah ﷻ in difficult times and easy times. That will reduce your worry and be more effective in gaining what you seek from your Hereafter. Know that the slave of Allah ﷻ has not achieved true contentment until his contentment in poverty and tribulation is like his contentment in affluence and ease. How can you make demands of Allah ﷻ in your matters? If you think His divine decree is contrary to your desires, then you are discontent! Maybe destruction awaited you had what you desired come to pass. But you are pleased when His divine decree compliments your desires! This is a result of the lack of your knowledge of the Unseen. How can you make demands if you are unfair like that? You have not been fair against yourself and you have not reached the door of contentment.

[CONTENTMENT AFTER ISTIKHĀRAH]

These are beautiful words. It means that when an individual seeks judgement from Allah ﷻ through *istikhārah*, he must then be content with what Allah ﷻ has chosen for him, whether it conforms to his desires or is at odds with it, because he has no idea which of the two is better for him. Also, Allah ﷻ cannot be blamed for His decree in this case, since His judgement was specifically sought.

For this reason, many of the early Muslims, such as Ibn Masʿud and others ﷺ, would command people, who are fearful they will not

1 Bayhaqī, *Shuʿab* (204).

bear patiently with Allah's choice when it contradicts their own, to also ask for well-being when they seek Allah's judgement, since He ﷻ might choose a tribulation for them which they will not endure. This has been related from the Prophet ﷺ, too, albeit with a weakness [in its chain of transmission].

It is related from Bakr al-Muzanī that a man would frequently seek the judgement of Allah ﷻ through *istikhārah* but was afflicted with trials. He became despondent and impatient, so Allah ﷻ revealed to one of the prophets ﷺ, 'Say to such slave of Mine, "If you are not one of those with firm resolution, then why not simply ask Me for well-being instead?"'

Tirmidhī and others have quoted in the hadith of Saʿd ﷺ that the Prophet ﷺ said,

إِنَّ مِنْ سَعَادَةِ الْمَرْءِ اسْتِخَارَتَهُ رَبَّهُ ﷻ وَرِضَاهُ بِمَا قَضَى، وَإِنَّ شَقَاوَتَهُ تَرْكُهُ الْإِسْتِخَارَةَ وَسَخَطُهُ بِمَا قَضَى.

> A sign of a person's good fortune is that he seeks the judgement of his Lord ﷻ through *istikhārah* and then is content with His decree. And a sign of a person's wretchedness is his refusal to seek the judgement of Allah ﷻ and he is discontent with His decree.[1]

CONTENTMENT WITH THE DIVINE DECREE

There are many ways of obtaining contentment with the divine decree. One of them is having certainty in Allah ﷻ and trusting that He ﷻ will only decree what is good for a believer, like a patient who has submitted to the well-wishing expert physician; he is content with anything he does to him—be it painful or otherwise—because of his trust and certainty that he only wants what is most beneficial for him. This is what Ibn ʿAwn was referring to in his previously-mentioned statement.

Another [means of attaining such a state] is concentrating on the

1 Tirmidhī (2151); Aḥmad (1444).

reward that Allah ﷻ has promised for contentment. The slave should immerse himself in that until he forgets the pain of what he is decreed, as is related about one the righteous women from the early Muslims. She fell and broke her nail and then laughed, saying, 'The pleasure of His reward has made me forget the bitterness of the pain.'

Yet another is—and it is the greatest of all of them—immersing oneself in the love of the One who afflicts, and forever observing His majesty, His beauty, His greatness and His perfection which have no end. The power of observing these leads to immersing oneself in Him until you feel no pain, much like the women who saw Yūsuf ﷷ; they were oblivious to the pain of cutting their hands because of seeing him.

Junayd said, 'I asked Sarī, "Does the lover feel the pain of affliction?" His response was, "No,"' which indicates his lofty station.

[We see another] example of this [state] in the following statement of many who were afflicted: 'He may do with us what He pleases. If He was to cut us into shreds, we would only increase in love for Him.'

One of them said something similar,

If love was to cut me piece by piece,
    The pain would only increase me in love.
I will always be a prisoner of love for You,
    Until I die, weeping from Your love.

Ibrāhīm ibn Adham left his kingdom, his wealth, his children and his entourage. His son saw him while in *ṭawāf* of the *Kaʿbah*, but he did not speak to him. So he said,

I flew away, abandoning creation in love for You,
    And I orphaned my family that I may see You.
If You were to cut me piece by piece for love,
    My heart would still not incline to anyone but You.

Many lovers of Allah ﷻ, like Fuḍayl and Fatḥ al-Mawṣilī, upon spending the night with no food nor light would become extremely happy and weep for joy, saying, 'The like of us, left without food or light! How did we achieve such a blessing? Through which plea did we gain such an honour?'

Fatḥ would gather his children in winter nights, wrapping them up in his mantle, saying, 'You have hungered me and hungered my family. You have impoverished me and impoverished my family. You only do that to Your friends and those You love. So [tell me], am I one of them, so that I may rejoice.'

Some people visited one of the early Muslims when he was sick. They asked him, 'What would you like?' He said, 'I would like what He likes.'

One of them said something similar,

Punishment for Your sake is pleasure
And distance for Your sake is closeness.
You are to me like my soul.
No, You are more beloved than it.
In love, it is suffices me that
I love that which You love.

Abū Turāb recited,

Do not be deceived, for the lover has proofs
And he has ways from the gifts of his Beloved.
Of them is his pleasure at bitter afflictions from Him
And expressing joy in all that He does.
Prohibition from Him is a welcome award,
For poverty is honour and a charitable gift is temporary.

A group visited a man whose son had been killed in jihad to offer him condolence. So he wept and said, 'I am not weeping because of his killing. I am weeping merely to know what the nature of his contentment with Allah ﷻ was when the sword struck him.'

If the dwellers of Ghadā are pleased
With my death, then so be it.
By Allah, I never felt hate
For the Beloved's wishes.

I have become their slave
And the slave cannot object.
They have rolled my heart,
Because of love, on embers of Ghadā.
Oh would that the fever-filled days
That passed come again!
Who is there for the ailing,
Who sees none but the attending physician?

[DIFFERENCE BETWEEN CONTENTMENT AND PATIENCE]

The main point is that the Prophet ﷺ commanded Ibn ʿAbbās ﷺ to act upon contentment, if he was able to. Then he ﷺ said to him, 'If you are not able to do so, then indeed there is much good that comes from patience upon what you dislike.'

This shows that being content with a painful decree is not an absolute necessity. It is merely a preferred excellence. Whoever is not able to be content should hold fast to patience, for patience is no doubt an obligation, and there is a great amount of good in it. Allah ﷻ commanded us to bear patiently, promising great reward for it, as He ﷻ says,

﴿إِنَّمَا يُوَفَّى الصَّابِرُونَ أَجْرَهُمْ بِغَيْرِ حِسَابٍ﴾

The patient will be paid their wages in full without any reckoning. (39:10)

And He ﷻ says,

﴿وَبَشِّرِ الصَّابِرِينَ ١٥٥ الَّذِينَ إِذَا أَصَابَتْهُمْ مُصِيبَةٌ قَالُوا إِنَّا لِلَّهِ وَإِنَّا إِلَيْهِ رَاجِعُونَ ١٥٦ أُولَٰئِكَ عَلَيْهِمْ صَلَوَاتٌ مِنْ رَبِّهِمْ وَرَحْمَةٌ وَأُولَٰئِكَ هُمُ الْمُهْتَدُونَ ١٥٧﴾

But give good news to the patient: those who, when disaster strikes them, say, 'We belong to Allah and to Him we will return.' Those are the people who will have blessings and mercy from their Lord; they are the ones who are guided. (2:155–157)

And He ﷻ says,

﴿وَبَشِّرِ الْمُخْبِتِينَ ۝٣٤ الَّذِينَ إِذَا ذُكِرَ اللَّهُ وَجِلَتْ قُلُوبُهُمْ وَالصَّابِرِينَ عَلَىٰ مَا أَصَابَهُمْ ۝٣٥﴾

Give good news to the humble-hearted, whose hearts quake at the mention of Allah, and who are patient in the face of all that happens to them. (22:34–35)

Ḥasan said, 'Contentment is honourable, but patience is a believer's responsibility.'

Sulaymān al-Khawwāṣ said, 'Patience is beneath contentment in rank. Contentment is when a person, even before hardship afflicts him, is content with whatever will happen; and patience is when he perseveres after hardships befall him.'

The reality of the difference between patience and contentment is [understood in the following terms]: patience is stopping and preventing the self from being displeased although pain is present. Contentment results in the expanding and spreading of the breast; and although one feels pain, the contentment lightens the feeling of pain. This [latter state] is due to the heart rejoicing through the spirit of certainty and recognition. Sometimes the feeling of pain is completely removed, according to what has already been mentioned.

This is why many of the early Muslims, such as ʿUmar ibn ʿAbd al-ʿAzīz, Fuḍayl, Abū Sulaymān, Ibn al-Mubārak and others, said, 'The content one does not wish for any other state than the one he is currently in, contrary to the patient one.'

This meaning—that they would not wish for any state other than the one they were currently in—has also been related from many Companions, such as ʿUmar and Ibn Masʿūd ﵄.

ʿAbd al-ʿAzīz ibn Abī Rawwād said,

> There was a worshipper from the Tribe of Isrāʾīl who devoted himself to worship. He saw in his dream that such-and-such woman would be his wife in Paradise. [Curious about her deed that granted her this,] he asked her to entertain him as her guest for three nights, so that he

> could see her deed. [Upon observing her, he saw that] she would sleep while he would stand in prayer, and she would eat while he would fast. When he parted from her, he asked her about the strongest deed that she does. She said, 'It is as you have seen, except for one trait: if I am experiencing a difficulty, I do not wish that I was in ease. If I have fallen ill, I do not wish to be healthy. If I am hungry, I do not wish to be satiated. And if I am in the sun, I do not wish to be in the shade.' The worshipper then said, 'This, by Allah, is a quality that slaves of Allah ﷻ are incapable of.'

Just as patience can only be at the first shock—as is authentically established from the Prophet ﷺ[1]—likewise contentment can only be once the trial has struck, as the Prophet ﷺ used to say in his supplication,

أَسْأَلُكَ الرِّضَا بَعْدَ الْقَضَاءِ.

> O Allah! I ask for contentment after the divine decree.[2]

This is so since the slave of Allah ﷻ is determined to be content before the divine decree occurs; but once it does occur, that determination weakens. So whoever is content after the occurrence of the divine decree is truly [to be considered] the content one.

In brief, patience is a necessary obligation, and anything short of it is displeasure. Whoever is displeased with the destiny of Allah ﷻ feels discontent in addition to the pain that has caught up with him. Enemies rejoicing at his misfortune is far worse than his grief, as some of the early Muslims have said,

> Worry not about every matter that befalls you,
> And look not at enemies who rejoice at your misfortune.
> O people! It is with patience that prizes are won.
> When you meet a troop, stand firm!

The Prophet ﷺ said,

---

1 Bukhārī (1302); Muslim (926).

2 Aḥmad (21666).

مَنْ يَتَصَبَّرْ يُصَبِّرْهُ اللهُ، وَمَا أُعْطِيَ أَحَدٌ عَطَاءً خَيْرًا وَأَوْسَعَ مِنَ الصَّبْرِ.

Whoever is patient, Allah ﷻ will make him forbearing. No one has been given a better and more generous gift than forbearance.[1]

ʿUmar ﷺ said, 'We found our best livelihood to be patience.'

ʿAlī ﷺ said, 'Patience in relation to belief is like the head in relation to the body. There is no belief for the one who has no patience.'

Ḥasan said, 'Patience is a treasure from the treasures of Paradise. Allah ﷻ does not give it to anyone except the one He has honoured.'

Maymūn ibn Mihrān said, 'No one—be he a prophet or otherwise—has received a great amount of good without patience.'

Ibrāhīm at-Taymī said, 'Whoever is given patience upon harm, patience upon trials and patience upon difficulties has been given the best thing that anyone has received after belief in Allah ﷻ.'

This is drawn from His ﷻ words,

﴿وَلَـٰكِنَّ الْبِرَّ مَنْ آمَنَ بِاللهِ وَالْيَوْمِ الْآخِرِ. . .وَالصَّابِرِينَ فِي الْبَأْسَاءِ وَالضَّرَّاءِ وَحِينَ الْبَأْسِ أُولَـٰئِكَ الَّذِينَ صَدَقُوا وَأُولَـٰئِكَ هُمُ الْمُتَّقُونَ﴾

Rather, those with true devoutness are those who believe. . .and are patient in poverty and illness and in battle. Those are the people who are true. They are the people who are God-fearing. (2:177)

The meaning of *ba'sā'* in this verse is poverty, and other such things, and *ḍarrā'* is illness and its like. *Ḥīna al-ba's* refers to jihad.

ʿUmar ibn ʿAbd al-ʿAzīz said, 'When Allah ﷻ bestows a blessing on a slave, then takes it from him and replaces it with patience, the replacement is better than what was taken away.' Then he recited,

﴿إِنَّمَا يُوَفَّى الصَّابِرُونَ أَجْرَهُم بِغَيْرِ حِسَابٍ﴾

The patient will be paid their wages in full without any reckoning. (39:10)

One of the early Muslims had a piece of paper which, from time to time, he would open and look at. In it was written,

1 Bukhārī (1469).

﴿وَاصْبِرْ لِحُكْمِ رَبِّكَ فَإِنَّكَ بِأَعْيُنِنَا﴾

So wait patiently for the judgement of your Lord—you are certainly before Our eyes. (52:48)

The best patience is when the slave conceals the difficulty and does not inform anyone of it. Many of the early pious Muslims said that having no complaints was the meaning of His ﷻ words,

﴿فَصَبْرٌ جَمِيلٌ﴾

But beauty lies in showing patience. (12:83)

Aḥnaf ibn Qays was blind for forty years, but he did not mention it to anyone. ʿAbd al-ʿAzīz ibn Abī Rawwād was blind for twenty years, and one day, his son looked attentively at him and said, 'My beloved father, your eyesight has gone!' He replied, 'Yes, my son. Your father's eyesight has been gone for twenty years, as a result of being content with Allah ﷻ.'

Imam Aḥmad would never complain to anyone about a sickness he had. It was mentioned to him that Mujāhid would dislike to groan in sickness, so he stopped it too, never to groan again until he died. He would say to himself, 'O self! Be patient! If you do not, you will regret it.'

One of the gnostics visited a sick person who said, 'Ahh!' So he said to him, 'Who are you complaining about?'

One of them used to say something with a similar meaning,

From souls emanate their hardships
　　Yet you conceal them from the visitors.
The soul has not been just in complaining
　　About its desires to other than its beloved.

Yaḥyā ibn Muʿādh said,

> If you love your Lord ﷻ and He starved you and stripped you of clothes, you would have to bear it and conceal it from creation, for indeed a

lover bears pain for his Beloved. How, then, can you complain to Him about something He has not done?

To me, an action not from You is unsightly
And if You do it, then they are beautiful.

The Prophet ﷺ and his Companions ﷺ would tie stones to their stomachs because of hunger.[1]

Uways would pick pieces of bread from the rubbish, competing with dogs to try and get it first. One day a dog barked at him, so he said,

O dog! Do not harm one who does not harm you. Eat what is on your side and I will eat what is on my side. If I enter Paradise, then I am better than you; but if I enter the Fire, then you are better than me.

Ibrāhīm ibn Adham would pick grains with the destitute. Forced to compete with him for the grains, they disapproved of his presence with them, so he thought to himself, 'I left the kingdom of Balkh only to compete with the poor in picking grains?' After that he only ever picked grains with the animals who grazed there. Imam Aḥmad too would pick grains with the destitute.

Sufyān ath-Thawrī once hired out his services for two camel drivers on the way to Makkah. He even cooked food for them, but [unintentionally] spoilt it, so they beat him.

Fatḥ al-Mawṣilī would light fires for people for a price.

For Your sake I have left my cheek on the ground
For the malicious and the envious ones, so that You are pleased.
My Master, until when will I enjoy these favours?
My life passes by and my need is not fulfilled.

Another poet said,

1 Bukhārī has recorded a hadith wherein Abū Hurayah ﷺ relates that he had to resort to this when he could not find food to eat (6452). Abū ʿAwānah has transmitted a hadith that states the Prophet ﷺ would also do this (6937).

Much pain and discomfort do I bear for Your love.
Much patience I have observed for you in sickness and grief.
Chase me not away for there is no availing against You,
And take my soul if You wish for payment.
Due to Your pleasure I have fallen in love
And my heart is enamoured and my tears will return.
For Your love, what I suffer is insignificant.
One who has not suffered cannot appreciate blessing.

The tribulations of the world were a blessing for them; so much so that one of them said, 'The one who does not see trials as a blessing and ease as a tribulation cannot be a man of deep understanding.'

It is mentioned in a Judaeo-Christian anecdote, 'When you see abundance coming, say, "This is punishment of a sin that has come early," and when you see poverty coming, say, "Welcome, O sign of the righteous!"'

One of the early Muslims said,

> If I am afflicted with a tribulation, I praise Allah ﷻ for it four times: I praise Allah ﷻ since it is not worse than it is; I praise Allah ﷻ for giving me patience in the face of it; I praise Him ﷻ for giving me the opportunity to say *istirjāʿ*[1] and I praise Him ﷻ for not making it in matters of my religion.

Waiting for salvation with patience is worship, for trials do not last forever:

Bear patiently in every affliction and be tough
And know that harm does not last forever.
Be patient as the honourable ones were patient,
A temporary calamity today will be removed tomorrow.

When the most afflicted person in the world plunges once into the

---

1 This refers to reciting the prayer prescribed in the Qur'an: *Those who, when disaster strikes them, say, 'Innā li'llāhi wa innā ilayhi rājiʿūn' (We belong to Allah and to Him we will return).* (2:156)

delights of Paradise, he will be asked, 'Did you ever feel distress? Did you ever suffer?' He will say, 'No, my Lord.'

> O self! It is nothing but patience for a few days,
>   Whose duration is like muddled dreams.
> O self! Pass by the world in haste
>   And leave it be, for livelihood lies ahead.

Another poet said,

> It is nothing but a moment which will pass
> And all this will disappear and cease to exist.

CHAPTER 10

Know That Victory Comes with Patience

This corresponds with His ﷻ words,

﴿يَاأَيُّهَا الَّذِينَ آمَنُوا إِذَا لَقِيتُمْ فِئَةً فَاثْبُتُوا وَاذْكُرُوا اللهَ كَثِيرًا لَعَلَّكُمْ
تُفْلِحُونَ﴾

O you who believe! When you meet a troop, stand firm and remember Allah repeatedly so that hopefully you will be successful. (8:45)

And His ﷻ words,

﴿فَإِنْ يَكُنْ مِنْكُمْ مِائَةٌ صَابِرَةٌ يَغْلِبُوا مِائَتَيْنِ وَإِنْ يَكُنْ مِنْكُمْ أَلْفٌ
يَغْلِبُوا أَلْفَيْنِ بِإِذْنِ اللهِ وَاللهُ مَعَ الصَّابِرِينَ﴾

If there are a hundred of you who are steadfast, they will overcome two hundred; and if there are a thousand of you, they will overcome two thousand with Allah's permission. Allah is with the patient. (8:66)

Then there are His ﷻ words in the story of Ṭālūt:

﴿فَلَمَّا جَاوَزَهُ هُوَ وَالَّذِينَ آمَنُوا مَعَهُ قَالُوا لَا طَاقَةَ لَنَا الْيَوْمَ بِجَالُوتَ وَجُنُودِهِ
قَالَ الَّذِينَ يَظُنُّونَ أَنَّهُمْ مُلَاقُو اللهِ كَمْ مِنْ فِئَةٍ قَلِيلَةٍ غَلَبَتْ فِئَةً كَثِيرَةً
بِإِذْنِ اللهِ وَاللهُ مَعَ الصَّابِرِينَ﴾

Then when he and those who believed with him had crossed it, they said, 'We do not have the strength to face Goliath and his troops today.' But those who were sure that they were going to meet Allah said, 'How many a small force has triumphed over a much greater one by Allah's permission!' Allah is with the patient. (2:249)

And His ﷻ words,

﴿بَلَىٰ إِنْ تَصْبِرُوا وَتَتَّقُوا وَيَأْتُوكُمْ مِنْ فَوْرِهِمْ هَٰذَا يُمْدِدْكُمْ رَبُّكُمْ بِخَمْسَةِ آلَافٍ مِنَ الْمَلَائِكَةِ مُسَوِّمِينَ﴾

Yes indeed! But if you are steadfast and fear Allah and they come upon you suddenly, your Lord will reinforce with 5000 angels, clearly identified. (3:125)

In fact, there are numerous other verses and hadiths commanding patience.

ʿUmar ﷺ said to the seniors from the tribe of ʿAbbās, 'What do you fight the people with?' They said, 'With patience. Whenever we meet a people, we are patient with them just as they are patient with us.'

One of the early Muslims said, 'Every one of us dislikes death and the pain of wounds but we excel each other through patience.'

Baṭṭāl was asked about courage and he said, 'It is patience, even for a moment.'

[PATIENCE IN JIHAD AGAINST THE SELF]

All of these verses and quotes are regarding jihad with the apparent enemy from among the unbelievers. However, it also applies to jihad with the hidden enemy, the self and its capricious desires. Fighting them is the greatest of jihads, as the Prophet ﷺ said,

الْمُجَاهِدُ مَنْ جَاهَدَ نَفْسَهُ لِلّٰهِ.

The warrior (*mujahid*) is the one who fights his self for the sake of Allah ﷻ.[1]

1 Tirmidhī (1621).

ʿAbdullāh ibn ʿAmr ؓ said to a man who asked him about jihad, 'Start with your self and fight it. Start with yourself and go to battle with it.'

It is related in the hadith of Jābir ؓ, with a weak chain of narration, that the Prophet ﷺ said to people who were returning from battle,

قَدِمْتُمْ مِنَ الْجِهَادِ الْأَصْغَرِ إِلَى الْجِهَادِ الْأَكْبَرِ. قِيلَ: وَمَا الْجِهَادُ الْأَكْبَرُ؟ قَالَ: مُجَاهَدَةُ الْعَبْدِ لِهَوَاهُ.

> You are returning from the minor jihad to the major jihad.' Someone asked, 'What is the major jihad?' He ﷺ said, 'A person's struggle with his desires.[1]

Abū Bakr aṣ-Ṣiddīq ؓ said to ʿUmar ؓ in his counsel when he appointed him as the Caliph, 'The first thing I warn you of is your ego [that hides] deep inside you.'

It is related in the hadith of Anas ؓ, from the Prophet ﷺ, and in the hadith of Abū Mālik al-Ashjaʿī, who narrates from the Prophet ﷺ—without the Companion in the chain—that he said,

لَيْسَ عَدُوُّكَ الَّذِي إِذَا قَتَلَكَ أَدْخَلَكَ الْجَنَّةَ، وَإِذَا قَتَلْتَهُ كَانَ لَكَ نُورًا، أَعْدَى عَدُوِّكَ نَفْسُكَ الَّتِي بَيْنَ جَنْبَيْكَ.

> Your enemy is not the one who kills you and enters you into Paradise, or the one whom you kill and you gain a light. Your worst enemy is your ego which is inside of you.[2]

ʿAbbās ibn al-Aḥnaf, the poet, has taken this very meaning when he said,

> My heart calls me to what will harm me
>   And what will increase my grief and pain.
> I so seldomly hold fast to my opinion,
>   I am on the verge of being lamented.[3]
> How do I guard against my enemy,
>   When my enemy lives inside me?

---

1 Bayhaqī, *az-Zuhd al-Kabīr* (373).

2 Ṭabarānī, *Kabīr* (3445).

3 I thank Moustafa Elqabbany for providing the translation of this middle part. [Ed.]

This jihad too requires patience. Whoever bears patiently when fighting his self, his desires and his shayṭān, he will be triumphant and victorious. And whoever is impatient and does not persevere when fighting them, he will be defeated, overwhelmed and imprisoned. He will be a disgraced prisoner in the hands of his shayṭān and his desires, as has been said:

> If one does not overcome his desires
> They will reduce the honourable to disgrace.

Another poet said,

> At times one is imprisoned by his passions
> But his patience appears and moves it aside.
> A man of desires is but a slave,
> But when he overcomes his desires, he is a king.

Ibn al-Mubārak said, 'How briefly the patient one had to bear patiently and how briefly the impatient one enjoyed himself!'

It is related in the *Ṣaḥīḥayn* from the Prophet ﷺ,

لَيْسَ الشَّدِيدُ بِالصُّرَعَةِ، إِنَّمَا الشَّدِيدُ الَّذِي يَمْلِكُ نَفْسَهُ عِنْدَ الغَضَبِ.

> The strong man is not the one who throws people down in wrestling. The strong man is the one who has control of himself when he is angry.[1]

Someone described Aḥnaf ibn Qays as 'the one who had the most authority over himself when he was angry.'

Someone once said, 'So-and-so walks on water.' So another person replied to him, 'The one whom Allah ﷻ has given strength to oppose his desires is mightier than the one who walks on water.'

Know that your self is like your animal; if it senses diligence in you, it will strive earnestly; and if it senses laziness from you, it will be greedy, and it will seek its pleasures and desires from you.

Abū Sulaymān ad-Dārānī would say,

1 Bukhārī (6114); Muslim (2609).

> While I was in Iraq, I was responsible for the palaces, the animals, the clothes and the food of the kings, but my self never turned to any of it. But when I was responsible for the dates, my self almost pounced on them.

That was mentioned to one of the gnostics who said, 'His self had no hope of getting the former, so it gave up; but it could have the latter, and so it desired it.'

This is as someone said,

> I was patient in refraining from pleasures until they left
> And I forced my self to leave them, so they stayed away.
> The self only goes where the young man points it.
> If it craves something, it will strive for it; and if not, it will turn away.
> For many days my self possessed power,
> But when it saw my determination for humility, it yielded.

So the words of the Prophet ﷺ, 'Victory comes with patience,' includes a person's jihad with the apparent enemy and his jihad with the hidden enemy, which is his self and his desires. The early Muslims would prefer the latter patience over patience in the face of difficulties.

Maymūn ibn Mijrān said, 'Patience is of two types: patience upon difficulty, which is good; and more virtuous than that is patience in refraining from sin.'

Saʿīd ibn Jubayr said,

> Patience has two parts: one is being patient in refraining from what Allah ﷻ has deemed unlawful and being patient in carrying out the worship that Allah ﷻ has obligated—which is the best form of patience; and the other is patience in difficulties.

The hadith of ʿAlī ﵁ from the Prophet ﷺ is also narrated regarding this, but it is not established.

CHAPTER 11

Relief Comes with Grief

This is confirmed by His ﷻ words,

﴿وَهُوَ الَّذِى يُنَزِّلُ الْغَيْثَ مِنْ بَعْدِ مَا قَنَطُوا﴾

It is He who sends down abundant rain, after they have lost all hope. (42:28)

Also His ﷻ words,

﴿اللهُ الَّذِى يُرْسِلُ الرِّيَاحَ فَتُثِيرُ سَحَابًا فَيَبْسُطُهُ فِي السَّمَاءِ كَيْفَ يَشَاءُ وَيَجْعَلُهُ كِسَفًا فَتَرَى الْوَدْقَ يَخْرُجُ مِنْ خِلَالِهِ فَإِذَا أَصَابَ بِهِ مَنْ يَشَاءُ مِنْ عِبَادِهِ إِذَا هُمْ يَسْتَبْشِرُونَ﴾

It is Allah who sends the winds which stir up clouds which He spreads about the sky however He wills. He forms them into dark clumps and you see the rain come pouring out from the middle of them. When He makes it fall on those of His slaves He wills, they rejoice. (30:48)

Imam Aḥmad has quoted the words of the Prophet ﷺ in the hadith of Abū Razīn al-ʿUqaylī,

ضَحِكَ رَبُّنَا مِنْ قُنُوطِ عِبَادِهِ وَقُرْبِ غِيَرِهِ.

> Our Lord laughs at the despair of His slaves and the proximity of his fate changing.[1]

Imam Aḥmad's son, ʿAbdullāh quotes the hadith of Abū Razīn too in the lengthy narration from the Prophet ﷺ,

عَلِمَ اللهُ يَوْمَ الْغَيْثِ إِنَّهُ لَيُشْرِفُ عَلَيْكُمْ آزِلِينَ قنطِينَ، فَيَظَلُّ يَضْحَكُ، قَدْ عَلِمَ أَنَّ غَيْرَكُمْ إِلَى قُرْبٍ.

> On the day of rainfall, Allah ﷻ knows that there will come upon you a state of despair, so He ﷻ is amused, knowing that a change of fate is soon at hand.[2]

This means that He ﷻ is delighted at His slaves' despair, fear, sorrow and loss of hope in mercy when He holds off the rain from them, although He has decreed that their situation is soon to change with rainfall, but they are unaware.

This is similar to the man's complaint to the Prophet ﷺ while he stood delivering a sermon on Friday about the lack of rain, causing people much trouble. So the Prophet ﷺ raised his hands and asked Allah ﷻ for rain for them until the clouds appeared. It continued to rain until the following Friday, when they stood before him, asking him to pray for the rain to stop. The Prophet ﷺ did so, and the heavens stopped raining.[3]

[STORIES ABOUT RELIEF AFTER GRIEF]

Allah ﷻ has related many stories in His Book, which discuss relief after grief and difficulties, like the deliverance of Nūḥ ﷺ—and that of those with him in the Ark—from the terrible plight, despite the drowning of everyone else on earth.

Similarly, He ﷻ related the deliverance of Ibrāhīm ﷺ from the fire, where the polytheists had flung him and the fact that He ﷻ made

1 Aḥmad (16201).
2 Aḥmad (16206).
3 Bukhārī (933); Muslim (897).

it cool and peaceful. Likewise, He related the story of Ibrāhīm with his son, whom he was commanded to slaughter, then Allah ransomed him with a mighty sacrifice.

Likewise, He related the story of Mūsā with his mother, when she placed him in the sea and the family of Pharaoh picked him up; and his story with Pharaoh, when Allah saved Mūsā in the sea and drowned his enemies.

Furthermore, there are the stories of Ayyūb, Yūnus, Yaʿqūb and the story of the people of Yūnus when they believed.

Moreover, Allah related the stories of Muhammad and his victory over his enemies; his deliverance from them on a number of occasions, like the story of him in the cave and his battles of Badr, Uḥud and Ḥunayn. In the same way, Allah related the story of ʿĀ'ishah in the incident of the Slander, exonerating her of what she was accused, as well as the story of the three [who missed the battle of Tabuk]:

﴿الَّذِينَ خُلِّفُوا حَتَّىٰ إِذَا ضَاقَتْ عَلَيْهِمُ الْأَرْضُ بِمَا رَحُبَتْ وَضَاقَتْ عَلَيْهِمْ أَنْفُسُهُمْ وَظَنُّوا أَنْ لَا مَلْجَأَ مِنَ اللهِ إِلَّا إِلَيْهِ ثُمَّ تَابَ عَلَيْهِمْ لِيَتُوبُوا﴾

Those who were left behind, so that when the earth became narrow for them, for all its great breadth, and their own selves became constricted for them and they realised that there was no refuge from Allah except in Him, He turned to them so that they might turn to Him. (9:118)

The Sunnah, in like manner, has a great deal of accounts of this nature, such as the story of the three who entered the cave and the boulder sealed them in. They supplicated to Allah through the medium of their righteous deeds, and He freed them.[1] Likewise, there is the story of Ibrāhīm and Sārah with the tyrant who sought her from Ibrāhīm, but Allah repelled the schemes of the degenerate.[2]

In addition, stories with this same meaning during Islam and prior to it are numerous, and closely examining all of them would not

1 Bukhārī (2272).

2 Bukhārī (3358); Muslim (2371).

be possible. Many of them are mentioned in books written on the topic of relief after grief by Ibn Abī 'd-Dunyā and others: in *Mujābī ad-Daʿwah* by Ibn Abī 'd-Dunyā, *al-Mustaghīthīn bi'llāh wa'l-Mustaṣrikhīn bihi*, books of the miracles of saints, stories of the righteous and history books etc.

We will mention here a small selection of the finest stories related on this topic so that lessons may be taken from them.

[A STOLEN POUCH]

One of the scholars—who I think was from North Africa—wrote that he heard Ḥāfiẓ Abū Dharr al-Harawī relating that he was in Baghdad, reciting to Abū Ḥafṣ ibn Shāhīn in a fragrance shop, when he saw a man come to the perfumer, give him ten dirhams and take his necessities from him. The man placed them in a tray, placed it on his head, but he slipped and the tray fell and his necessities scattered everywhere. So he wept and wept profusely and said,

> I once lost a pouch containing four hundred dinars—or he said four thousand dinars—with precious stones worth just as much in such-and-such caravan. I did not mourn when I lost that, but a child has been born to me last night and we needed things in the house that a woman in post-childbirth usually requires. I had nothing but these ten dirhams, and so when Allah ﷻ decreed what He decreed, I became worried. I said to myself that I have nothing to take home to my family nor anything to earn for them tomorrow. I have no other option but to abandon them and leave them in this state to die in my absence; hence, I could not control myself from mourning like this.

Abū Dharr continued to say,

> Meanwhile, there was an old soldier from the army, sitting at the door, who heard all of that. The soldier asked Abū Ḥafṣ if he could invite him, his companions and the grief-stricken person into his house, and he did so. He then asked the grief-stricken man to repeat the story of

> the pouch, and he did so. He asked about that caravan and the place where he lost the pouch, so he informed him. Then he asked him to describe the pouch and its markings, so he told him. He then said, 'Would you recognise it if you saw it?' He replied, 'Yes!' He then took it out and when he saw it he said, 'This is the pouch I dropped and it has the stones I described as such!' He opened the pouch and found the stones as he described. So he returned it to him and left, and the man became rich.
>
> When the man left, the old soldier wept profusely. He was asked why he was weeping, so he said, 'I had no other hope nor wish in this world except for Allah ﷻ to bring to me the owner of this wealth to reclaim his property. Now that Allah ﷻ, by His Grace, has fulfilled that and I have no other wish, I know that my time has come.'

Abū Dharr said, 'Not a month had passed before he died and we offered the funeral prayer for him.'

[THE MERCHANT'S WEALTH]

The same author also writes that in Mosul, there was a man who was with a merchant, who would travel to other lands with his merchandise. On one occasion, he travelled to Kufa with all his wealth and everything he owned. On that journey, he chanced upon a man who served him generously and they became friends, and eventually he came to trust him. Once they stopped to camp and he distracted him, and he took off with his animal and all the wealth and belongings on it, leaving nothing at all. He tried to look for him but found no sign of him, so he returned to his city on foot and starving. He entered the city at night and in this state he knocked his door. When his family found out he had returned they were overjoyed and said,

> All praise is for Allah who brought you at this time. Your wife has given birth today and we have nothing with which to buy necessities for a woman in post-childbirth. She is extremely hungry tonight, so buy flour and oil for us to light a lamp.

When he heard that, it increased his grief and his worry. He did not want to tell them about what the unfortunate incident and grieve them too, so he went out to a shop close to his home. He greeted the owner and took oil and other necessities from him. While he was talking to him, he suddenly turned and saw his saddlebag which his servant had fled with lying on the floor of the shop. So he asked him about it and he responded,

> A man came here after nightfall and he purchased some supper from me. He asked me to host him, so I did. He then placed his saddlebag in my shop, left his animal in our neighbour's house and went to spend the night in the masjid.

So he got up to go to the masjid with the saddlebag, and he found the man sleeping there. He kicked him, awaking and startling him. He asked him, 'Where is my wealth, traitor?' He replied, 'It is there around your neck! By Allah, you will not find anything missing from it!' So he took his animal from where it was and gave his family what they needed. Only then did he tell about what had transpired.

[THE BAGHDADI WHO SACRIFICED FOR LOVE]

Tanūkhī mentions a similar story in his book. The story is very lengthy but this is its summary: There was a man, a treasurer who lived in Baghdad during the time of Rashīd. Once, he bought a maid for five hundred dinars. Falling deeply in love with her, he abandoned his livelihood to stay with her, even spending the last of his capital until none of it was left. His maid became pregnant, so he began tearing down his home to sell pieces of it until none of it remained. When her labour pains started, she asked him to purchase some necessities for after childbirth. She complained to him that she would die if he did not hurry with these things. Hopeless, he wept and left in that state. He had no idea what to do, so he contemplated drowning himself in the River Dajlah, but then feared the punishment of Allah ﷻ and desisted. He walked from town to town on foot until he reached

Khorasan, settling there and earning some money. He had written sixty-six letters to his city enquiring about his maid, but no reply came back, so he was certain she had died.

Then, after a long while, he returned to Baghdad with wealth worth 20,000 dinars, but thieves attacked his caravan and took everything he had. Thus, he was once again a poor man, with only the clothes on his back. He pressed on, heading for Baghdad until he finally arrived, but as a poor man, just as he had left, after being away for thirty-odd years! He made his way home and found it repaired and its gate was intact. Standing there he found a gatekeeper, two children and a mule driver, so he asked them about the house, 'Who does it belong to?' He was told, 'It belongs to the son of such-and-such treasurer,' taking his own name. They said, 'He is the son of the midwife of the Leader of the Believers. He is his accountant and deals with his wealth.' He then related what his father had told him about the owner of the house:

> The father of this man—in other words, the actual man of the house—was a great treasurer but fell to poverty, and the mother of his child was in labour, so his father left to look for something for her. However, he went missing and died. His mother sent word to a neighbour, asking them for help and they tended to her post-childbirth needs. Furthermore, a son was born to the Leader of the Believers. That son—who is Ma'mūn—was presented with every wet nurse, but he did not accept their milk until they were directed to the mother of this child, and she was taken to the house of Rashīd. The baby boy placed his mouth on her and right away he accepted her and suckled. She became very honoured among them. When Ma'mūn became the Caliph, the woman and her son were with him and her son built this house.

He then asked him about the mother, 'Is she alive?' They responded, 'Yes. Some days she goes to the house of the Caliph and other days she stays with her son.'

The treasurer made his way to the house and entered along with others, and he saw her in utmost beauty. He also saw sitting by her a young man who resembled him. In front of him was a book, money and weighing scales, where they gave and took money. The man sat among the crowd of the people until they left and no one remained but him. So the youngster asked him, 'Old man, do you need something?' He replied, 'Yes. I am your father!' His face changed and he hurriedly leapt forward. He invited him to his house and sat him down on a chair where there was a veil. The old man said to him, 'Perhaps you will want to verify the truth of my claim with so-and-so,' naming his maid—the mother of his child. The maid heard his voice and she lifted the veil. She came out to her former master, kissing him and weeping. He informed her of his ordeal from the moment he left her until his return. At that moment, his son stood up and apologised for his shortcomings and put things right with him. Then he took him and related his story to Ma'mūn, who bestowed him with a robe of honour and made him his treasurer, like his son was before. He gave him plentiful provisions and promoted his son to an even greater office than his.

[SAWWĀR AND THE BLIND MAN]

Muᶜāfī ibn Zakariyyā an-Nahrawānī relates with a chain of narration from Sawwār al-Qāḍī that one day, he left the house of Mahdī and went home. He asked for his food but it did not sit well with his stomach, so he sent it back. He then called his maid but realised he was not in the mood for company. Eventually, he went to take a siesta but could not sleep, so he got up and mounted his mule. Thereafter, he met one of his clerks who had two thousand dirhams, so he said to him, 'Hold on to it and come with me,' so he left his mule and went with him. It was the time for prayer when he was on some street, so he entered a masjid there and prayed. Once he had finished his prayer, he noticed a blind man looking for something, so he asked him, 'What do you want?' He responded, 'I want you.' So he asked, 'What do you need?' He responded, 'I smelt a sweet fragrance from you and assumed you to be a rich person, so I wanted to make a request.' He said, 'Speak.' He began, 'Do you see this palace here?' to which the man said, 'Yes.' He carried on, 'It belonged to my father who then sold it. He and I left for Khorasan, but we lost all our wealth. Now, I have come to speak to the owner of the house to request him to help me find and get in touch with Sawwār, since he is a friend of my father.' Sawwār said,

> I asked him who his father was and he said, 'So-and-so, son of so-and-so.' He was one of my closest friends, so I said to him, "Indeed, Allah ﷻ has brought Sawwār to you. He did not let him eat, drink or sleep and He has brought him right in front of you.'

Sawwār then called his clerk, took an amount of dirhams from him and gave them to the man. He said to him, 'Come to me tomorrow.' Sawwār said, 'I went to see Mahdī and I related to him this incident.' Mahdī was very pleased and he ordered for two thousand dirhams to be given to the blind man and a hundred thousand dinars to Sawwār. Sawwār said, 'When the blind man came to me, I gave him two thousand dirhams and said to him, "Allah ﷻ, through His generosity, has provided you with much good and you have been given two thousand dinars of my wealth too."'

[Waḍḍāḥ's Escape from Death]

Ibn Abī 'd-Dunyā has quoted in his book, *al-Faraj baʿd ash-Shiddah*, with a chain of narration from Waḍḍāḥ ibn Khaythamah, who said,

> Umar ibn ʿAbd al-ʿAzīz ordered me to release some prisoners, so I released them, all except Yazīd ibn Abī Muslim, who swore to kill me. Later, [when Yazīd was free] and I was in North Africa, I was told that Yazīd had come as the governor of North Africa, so I fled from him. He sent a party to find me and finally, I was gripped and taken to him. He said to me, 'By Allah, long have I asked Allah to bring me to you!' I said, 'By Allah, me too! How long I have sought Allah's refuge

> from your evil.' He said, 'By Allah, He has not given you refuge. By Allah, I will surely kill you, then, by Allah, I will kill you again and again. If the Angel of Death was to race with me to capture your soul, I would overtake him [by killing you first]. Bring me the sword and the execution mat!

He then said,

> The mat was brought, and I sat on it shackled. Someone stood at my head with a drawn sword, but the prayer was about to begin, so he left for the prayer. When he was in prostration, some soldiers struck him with their swords, killing him instantly. A man came to me and cut my shackles with his sword and said, 'Go!'

[ʿUMAR AS-SARĀYĀ AND THE BYZANTINE]

He has also quoted with a chain of narration from ʿUmar as-Sarāyā that he was by himself while on a military expedition in the land of the Byzantines. One day, while he was sleeping, a byzantine walked over to him and, prodding him with his foot, woke him up. He said, 'Arab! Choose whichever you wish: a duel with spears, a sword fight or a wrestling contest.' I said, 'There is no chance of survival with spears and swords. So let us wrestle.' So he dismounted, wrestled me to the ground and sat on my chest and said, 'How should I kill you?' I then lifted my head and prayed, 'I bear witness that anything that is worshipped beneath Your Throne and above the ground is false, except for Your Honourable Face. You see my predicament, so save me!' He said that he himself fell unconscious and when he regained his senses, the Byzantine was lying dead next to him.

[ḤĀTIM AL-AṢAMM AND THE TURK]

Abū 'l-Ḥasan ibn al-Jahḍam related with his chain of narration from Ḥātim al-Aṣamm that he said,

> Once, we met the Turks and had a contest with them. A Turk threw me, dropping me from my horse, then he got down and sat on my chest, gripping my beard in his hand and taking a knife out of his sock to kill me. My heart was not concerned with him nor his knife, but it was with my Master. So I said, 'My Master! If you have decreed for this person to kill me, then I am at Your service. I belong only to You and I am Your property.' While I was in this state, a Muslim threw a spear at him, piercing his neck. He fell off me, so I stood over him, took the knife from his hand and killed him with it. Only when your hearts are with the Master will you see wonders of His kindness; the kind you will not see from fathers and mothers!

This is a topic that can be extremely lengthy to cover, but we will suffice on these incidents.

CHAPTER 12

With Hardship Comes Ease

This is extracted from His ﷻ words,

﴿سَيَجْعَلُ اللهُ بَعْدَ عُسْرٍ يُسْرًا﴾

Allah will appoint ease after difficulty. (65:7)

And His ﷻ words,

﴿فَإِنَّ مَعَ الْعُسْرِ يُسْرًا ۝٥ إِنَّ مَعَ الْعُسْرِ يُسْرًا ۝٦﴾

For indeed with hardship comes ease. Indeed, with hardship comes ease. (94:5–6)

Ḥumayd ibn Ḥammād ibn Abū 'l-Khawwār relates,

'Ā'idh ibn Shurayḥ narrated to us that he heard Anas ibn Mālik رضي الله عنه saying,

كَانَ النَّبِيُّ ﷺ جَلِسًا وَحِيَالَهُ جُحْرٌ فَقَالَ: لَوْ جَاءَ الْعُسْرُ فَدَخَلَ هَذَا الْجُحْرَ لَجَاءَ الْيُسْرُ حَتَّى يَدْخُلَ عَلَيْهِ فَيُخْرِجَهُ، فَأَنْزَلَ اللهُ ﷻ: ﴿فَإِنَّ مَعَ الْعُسْرِ يُسْرًا ۝٥ إِنَّ مَعَ الْعُسْرِ يُسْرًا ۝٦﴾

The Prophet ﷺ was sitting in front of a hole and he said, 'If hardship was to come and enter this hole, ease would follow it and

> bring it out.' Then Allah ﷻ revealed, *For indeed with hardship comes ease. Indeed, with hardship comes ease* (94:5–6).[1]

Ibn Abī Ḥātim has quoted this in his *Tafsīr*, as has Bazzār in his *Musnad*. The latter has this variation:

لَوْ جَاءَ الْعُسْرُ حَتَّى يَدْخُلَ هَذَا الْجُحْرَ لَجَاءَ الْيُسْرُ حَتَّى يُخْرِجَهُ ثُمَّ قَالَ: ﴿إِنَّ مَعَ الْعُسْرِ يُسْرًا﴾

> 'If hardship was to come and enter this hole, ease would come and take it out.' Then he ﷺ said, '*Indeed, with hardship comes ease.*' (94:5–6)[2]

Ḥumayd ibn Ḥammād (in this chain) has been considered weak in hadith.

Ibn Abī Ḥātim quotes from the narration of Mubārak ibn Fuḍālah, who relates that Ḥasan ﵀ said, 'People used to say, "One hardship will not overcome two eases."'[3]

Ibn Jarīr quotes from the narration of Maʿmar who relates that Ḥasan said,

خَرَجَ النَّبِيُّ ﷺ يَوْمًا مَسْرُورًا فَرِحًا وَهُوَ يَقُولُ: لَنْ يَغْلِبَ عُسْرٌ يُسْرَيْنِ، لَنْ يَغْلِبَ عُسْرٌ يُسْرَيْنِ ﴿فَإِنَّ مَعَ الْعُسْرِ يُسْرًا ۝٥ إِنَّ مَعَ الْعُسْرِ يُسْرًا ۝٦﴾

> 'The Prophet ﷺ came out one day extremely happy, saying, "One hardship will never overcome two eases. One hardship will never overcome two eases. *For indeed with hardship comes ease. Indeed, with hardship comes ease.*" (94:5–6)'[4]

He has also quoted it from the narration of ʿAwf and Yūnus who relate it from Ḥasan with a missing link in the chain, and from the narration of Qatādah who said, 'It has been mentioned to us that the Messenger

---

1 Ḥākim (3010).
2 Ibn Abī Ḥātim (19395); Bazzār (7530).
3 Ibn Abī Ḥātim (19396).
4 Ṭabarī, 24:495.

of Allah ﷺ gave glad tidings to his Companions ﷺ with this verse[1] and then said, "One hardship will never overcome two eases."'

Ibn Abī 'd-Dunyā relates from the hadith of Muʿāwiyah ibn Qurrah who was informed by someone that Ibn Masʿūd ﷺ said, 'If hardship was to enter a hole, ease would follow it.' Then he said, 'Allah ﷺ says, *For indeed with hardship comes ease. Indeed, with hardship comes ease.*'

He also relates from the hadith of ʿAbd ar-Raḥmān ibn Zayd ibn Aslam, who relates from his father, who relates from his grandfather that Abū ʿUbaydah ﷺ was under siege, so ʿUmar ﷺ wrote to him, saying,

> No difficulty ever befalls a person except that Allah ﷺ facilitates deliverance for him after it. Indeed, one hardship will never overcome two eases. Indeed, He ﷺ says,
>
> ﴿اصْبِرُوا وَصَابِرُوا وَرَابِطُوا وَاتَّقُوا اللَّهَ لَعَلَّكُمْ تُفْلِحُونَ﴾
>
> *Be patient, be supreme in patience, be firm on the battlefield, and have fear of Allah, so that hopefully you will be successful.* (3:200)

Similarly, Ibn ʿAbbās ﷺ and other exegetes have said regarding this verse, 'One hardship will never overcome two eases.'

One of the predecessors was overcome with sheer grief during the night while he was in the desert. In his fright, he recited a couplet:

I see death is far better
    For the one who is afraid.
Then, when darkness fell, he heard a voice say,
    Listen, you man
Who has been troubled by grief!
    He has recited a couplet
Which continues to come to his mind.
    When your hardship becomes fierce
Ponder over *Did we not expand for you?*[2]
    So one hardship between two eases,
When you see it you will rejoice.

---

1 Qur'an 94:5–6.

2 Qur'an 94:1.

He said, 'I memorised the couplets and Allah ﷻ dispelled my grief.'

[POEMS ABOUT HARDHSIP AND EASE]

Poets have composed many couplets on this subject, some of which we will mention. These are a sample selected from the best of what has been said on this topic:

> Bear patiently for the outcome of patience is best
> And do not mourn with the strike of misfortune.
> Ease, after hardship, will indeed come
> And troubles, at the point of difficulty, will disappear.

One of them said,

> How many a person has become unhappy
> With a thing to be followed swiftly by deliverance!

Another said,

> Perhaps deliverance is at hand.
> Perhaps we entertain the thought of 'hopefully'.
> The closest a person is to deliverance
> Is when he about to lose hope.

Someone else said,

> When matters become difficult, wait for deliverance
> For the most difficult matters are closest to salvation.

One of them said,

> Do not mourn, even if you are poor one day,
> For you have been living easily for a longer time.
> Never have a bad opinion of your Lord
> For Allah is more deserving of good.

Do not be despondent, since losing hope is disbelief.
    Maybe Allah will enrich you very soon.
For indeed hardship is pursued by ease
    And it is said: Allah is the Most Truthful in what is said.

Another said,

Patience is the key to the gate of deliverance
    And every hardship is followed by ease.
Time does not stick to one condition
    Since one situation is followed another.

Another one of them said,

When hearts are overcome with despair
    And the care-free heart is now confined because of it;
When calamities are settled and have found their footing
    And they have dropped their afflictions in their places;
When you see no way to remove the harm
    And your resourceful life is of no avail;
Help will come to you despite your hopelessness,
    Bestowed by the Most Kind, the One who readily answers.
Every calamity, even if it has reached its peak,
    Is indeed joined with deliverance close at hand.

One of them said,

Perhaps what you see will not last forever.
    Perhaps you will see salvation from the clamour of time.
Perhaps Allah will bring deliverance.
    Every day He is engaged in affairs of His creation.
When hardship emerges, hope for ease,
    For Allah decreed that hardship is followed by ease.

[*Wisdom of Tribulations*]

We intend to end this book by presenting a short section on the subtleties of tribulations and their benefits and multi-faceted wisdoms:

FIRST: Sins are written off through tribulations, and one is rewarded for being patient during them. There is a difference of opinion among the scholars as to whether one is rewarded merely by being subject to tribulations or not.

SECOND: The slave of Allah ﷻ becomes aware of his sins through tribulations, sometimes causing him to relent and return to Allah ﷻ.

THIRD: Hardness of the heart is removed and it starts to become soft.

One of the early Muslims said, 'Sometimes a slave becomes sick, so he remembers his sins and fears Allah ﷻ, [only very little though-] to the amount of a flea's head, but Allah ﷻ still forgives him.'

FOURTH: The slave of Allah ﷻ stands before Him, humbled and defeated. That is more beloved to Allah ﷻ than many acts of obedience.

FIFTH: Tribulations require the slave of Allah ﷻ to return to him with his heart and stand at His door, humbling himself and begging before Him. That is the greatest benefit of tribulations, and Allah ﷻ has even rebuked those who do not lower themselves before Him at times of difficulty. Allah ﷻ says,

﴿وَلَقَدْ أَخَذْنَاهُم بِالْعَذَابِ فَمَا اسْتَكَانُوا لِرَبِّهِمْ وَمَا يَتَضَرَّعُونَ﴾

> *We seized them with the punishment, but they did not go low before their Lord; nor will they humble themselves.* (23:76)

And He ﷻ says,

﴿وَلَقَدْ أَرْسَلْنَا إِلَىٰ أُمَمٍ مِنْ قَبْلِكَ فَأَخَذْنَاهُمْ بِالْبَأْسَاءِ وَالضَّرَّاءِ لَعَلَّهُمْ يَتَضَرَّعُونَ﴾

> *We sent messengers to nations before you, and afflicted those nations with hardship and distress so that hopefully they would humble themselves.* (6:42)

It is mentioned in one of the earlier scriptures that Allah ﷻ tries His slave because He loves to hear him begging. Saʿīd ibn ʿAbd al-ʿAzīz relates that Dāwūd ﷺ said, 'Pure is He, who brings out supplication from tribulations! Pure is He, who brings out thankfulness from times of ease!'

Abū Jaʿfar Muhammad ibn ʿAlī once passed by Muhammad ibn al-Munkadir, who was sat sorrowful. He asked why he was sad and was told, 'He is drowning in debt.' So Abū Jaʿfar asked, 'Shall I implore for him in supplication?' and he was told, 'Yes.' He then said, 'A slave is blessed more when he is in difficulty than when he supplicates to his Lord—whatever the supplication may be.'

One of the early Muslims, when someone would implore Allah ﷻ for him in supplication during his times of difficulty, would not want it to be accepted quickly for fear of losing the tribulation.

Thābit said, 'When the believer supplicates to Allah ﷻ, He appoints Jibrīl ﷺ to tend to his need and says, "Do not be hasty in answering him, for I love to hear the voice of My believing slave."' This has also been related from the Prophet ﷺ, albeit through weak chains.[1]

One of the early Muslims saw the Lord of Might in his dream, so he asked him, 'My Lord! How often I supplicate to You but You do not answer me!' He ﷻ said, 'I love to hear your voice.'

SIXTH: Tribulations create a pleasurable taste for patience and

---

1 Ṭabarānī, *Awsaṭ* (8442).

contentment in the heart. This is truly a great station, and we have already pointed out its excellence and honour.

SEVENTH: Tribulations prevent a believer's heart from turning to creation, forcing them to turn to the Creator ﷻ alone. Allah ﷻ has mentioned the sincere supplications of a polytheist at times of difficulty,[1] so what of the believer? Tribulations, therefore, necessitate verification of Allah's oneness in His slave's heart. That is the loftiest station and the noblest position.

It is mentioned in Judaeo-Christian anecdotes that Allah ﷻ says, 'Tribulations bring Me and you together, whereas well-being brings you and your self together.'

1 Qur'an 10:22–23 and 29:65.

Conclusion

When troubles are intense and circumstances agonising, at that moment deliverance is usually close at hand. Allah ﷻ says,

﴿حَتَّىٰ إِذَا اسْتَيْأَسَ الرُّسُلُ وَظَنُّوا أَنَّهُمْ قَدْ كُذِبُوا جَاءَهُمْ نَصْرُنَا﴾

Then when the messengers despaired and thought themselves denied, Our help came to them. (12:110)

And He ﷻ says,

﴿مَسَّتْهُمُ الْبَأْسَاءُ وَالضَّرَّاءُ وَزُلْزِلُوا حَتَّىٰ يَقُولَ الرَّسُولُ وَالَّذِينَ آمَنُوا مَعَهُ
مَتَىٰ نَصْرُ اللَّهِ أَلَا إِنَّ نَصْرَ اللَّهِ قَرِيبٌ﴾

Poverty and illness afflicted them and they were shaken to the point that the Messenger and those who believed with him said, 'When is Allah's help coming?' Be assured that indeed Allah's help is very near. (2:214)

Allah ﷻ relates that Yaʿqūb ﷷ never lost hope in meeting Yūsuf ﷷ again, telling his other sons,

﴿اذْهَبُوا فَتَحَسَّسُوا مِنْ يُوسُفَ وَأَخِيهِ وَلَا تَيْأَسُوا مِنْ رَوْحِ اللَّهِ إِنَّهُ لَا
يَيْأَسُ مِنْ رَوْحِ اللَّهِ إِلَّا الْقَوْمُ الْكَافِرُونَ﴾

Seek news of Yūsuf and his brother. Do not despair of solace from Allah. Indeed, no one despairs of solace from Allah except for people who are unbelievers. (12:87)

He ﷷ also said,

﴿عَسَى اللَّهُ أَنْ يَأْتِيَنِي بِهِمْ جَمِيعًا﴾

Perhaps Allah will bring them all together. (12:83)

A subtle underlying reason for the coupling of deliverance with difficulties is that when troubles are intense and agonising, a person feels hopeless in the creation, removing himself from them, and he secures a connection with the Creator ﷻ alone. Whoever severs the link with creation and connects with the Creator will surely be answered by Allah ﷻ, and He will remove his difficulties. Reliance is to stop looking to creation by losing hope in them, as Imam Aḥmad said. To prove his point, he uses the statement of Ibrāhīm ﵇ when Jibrīl ﵇ appeared before him [as he was flung] in the air and asked, 'Do you have any need?' He ﵇ responded, 'From you? No.'[1]

Reliance is one of the greatest ways to seek one's needs, since Allah ﷻ suffices for the one who relies on Him, as He ﷻ says,

﴿وَمَنْ يَتَوَكَّلْ عَلَى اللَّهِ فَهُوَ حَسْبُهُ﴾

Whoever puts his trust in Allah, He will be enough for him. (65:3)

Fuḍayl said, 'By Allah! If you were to lose all hope in creation, to the point where you want nothing from them, your Master will give you all that you want.'

Another fundamental reason is that when troubles are intense for the slave of Allah ﷻ, he needs to struggle against Shayṭān at that very moment. Shayṭān comes to him and tries to embitter him and drive him to despair, so the slave must struggle against him and repel him. Thereafter, the reward of his struggle and vanquishing his enemy is that the tribulation is removed.

This is why it is mentioned in the authentic hadith,

يُسْتَجَابُ لِأَحَدِكُمْ مَا لَمْ يُعَجِّلْ، فَيَقُولُ: دَعَوْتُ فَلَمْ يُسْتَجَبْ لِي، فَيَدَعُ الدُّعَاءَ.

---

1 Bayhaqī, *Shuʿab al-Īmān* (10:45).

> The supplication of anyone of you will be answered, as long as he is not hasty, complaining, "I asked but was not answered," and then he leaves supplication.[1]

In addition, when the believer has waited a long time for deliverance and begins to lose hope in it—especially after many humble supplications and no sign of an answer—he turns to himself in blame and says, 'It is because of you that I have been made to suffer. Had there been some good in you, you would have been answered.'

This reproach is more beloved to Allah ﷻ than many forms of obedience, since it requires the slave of Allah ﷻ to be heartbroken before his Master, admitting to Him that his supplication is not worthy of response. For this reason, at this moment, his supplication is promptly accepted, and he is delivered from the tribulation. This is due to the fact that Allah ﷻ is with those whose hearts are broken because of Him. His power will be in proportion to the extent of one's broken-heartedness.

Wahb said,

> A man worshipped for a long time, then a need arose for [him that he had to place before] Allah ﷻ. Hence he fasted seventy Saturdays and ate only eleven dates on those Saturdays. Thereafter, he asked Allah ﷻ for his need, but he was not given it, so he turned to himself and said, 'This has happened because of you. If there was any good in you, you would have received your need.' At that moment an angel descended and said, 'Man! This moment of yours is better than all your past worship. Now Allah has fulfilled your need.'

I humble my self for them that they may honour it.
The self which is not humbled can never be honoured.

Whoever realises this, will understand it and witness it with his heart; he will know that Allah's ﷻ blessings upon His believing slave during tribulations is greater than His blessings during times of ease. This is the realisation of the authentic hadith from the Prophet ﷺ,

---

1 Bukhārī (6340); Muslim (2735).

لَا يَقْضِي اللهُ لِلْمُؤْمِنِ قَضَاءً إِلَّا كَانَ خَيْرًا لَهُ، إِنْ أَصَابَتْهُ سَرَّاءُ فَشَكَرَ كَانَ خَيْرًا لَهُ، وَإِنْ أَصَابَتْهُ ضَرَّاءُ صَبَرَ كَانَ خَيْرًا لَهُ، وَلَيْسَ ذَلِكَ إِلَّا لِلْمُؤْمِنِ.

Allah ﷻ does not decree a matter for a believer except that it is good for him. If good fortune comes to him, he is thankful, and that is good for him; and if difficulty befalls him, he is patient, and that is good for him. That is not for anyone but the believer.[1]

For this reason, the gnostics of Allah ﷻ did not like to choose one state over the other. Whichever Allah ﷻ decreed for them, they were pleased with it and worshipped Allah ﷻ accordingly.

It is related in the *Musnad* and mentioned by Tirmidhī from Abū Umāmah ؓ that the Prophet ﷺ said,

عَرَضَ عَلَيَّ رَبِّي لِيَجْعَلَ لِي بَطْحَاءَ مَكَّةَ ذَهَبًا فَقُلْتُ: لَا يَا رَبِّ، وَلَكِنْ أَشْبَعُ يَوْمًا وَأَجُوعُ يَوْمًا، فَإِذَا جُعْتُ تَضَرَّعْتُ إِلَيْكَ وَذَكَرْتُكَ، وَإِذَا شَبِعْتُ شَكَرْتُكَ وَحَمِدْتُكَ.

My Lord offered to turn the valley of Makkah to gold for me, but I said, 'No, my Lord! Rather, I will be satiated for a day and remain hungry for a day. When I am hungry, I will be humbled before You, and I will remember You; and when I am satiated, I will thank You and praise You.'[2]

ʿUmar ؓ said, 'I care not if morning finds me in a circumstance pleasing to me or in a circumstance I dislike, for I know not if there is good in what pleases me or in what displeases me.'

O so-and-so! Why, when We call you to Us, do you flee from Us? We shower you with blessings, yet you preoccupy yourself with them and forget Us! So we will let loose tribulations on you so that you will return to Us! And you will stand at Our door, and We will hear your begging! Tribulations bring Us and you together, while well-being only brings you together with your ego!

---

1 Muslim relates a variation of this hadith (2999).

2 Aḥmad (22190); Tirmidhī (2347).

If there is reproach between us
    Or our homes are far away,
The love you pledged will still prevail
    And the help you promised will be plentiful.
How many of our blessings are hidden in calamities
    And how many a gift is concealed in seclusion!

O so-and-so! If you are thankful for Our blessings, then you being thankful is the sum of Our blessings, so be thankful for that too! If you are patient upon Our tribulations, then that patience too is the sum of Our blessings, so remember it! Whatever you find yourself in is from Our blessings, so do not be ungrateful for it!

﴿وَإِنْ تَعُدُّوا نِعْمَتَ اللهِ لَا تُحْصُوهَا﴾

If you tried to number Allah's blessings, you could never count them. (14:34)

If I am thankful for my blessings,
    Then that too requires thankfulness.
How can there be thankfulness without His wish,
    Though days are long and life carries on?
When good fortune comes, all celebrate it,
    And if adversity strikes, reward follows it.
In each of he two, there are His blessings
    That cannot be restricted by imagination, land or sea.

I praise Allah upon completing the book, through His favour, His generosity and His splendid facilitation.

Bibliography

Abdel Haleem, M. A. S. *The Qur'an: A New Translation*. Oxford: Oxford University Press, 2004.

Abū Dāwūd, Sulaymān ibn Ashʿath. *Sunan Abī Dāwūd*. Beirut: al-Maktabah al-ʿAṣriyyah, n.d.

Abū Nuʿaym, Aḥmad ibn ʿAbdillāh al-Iṣbahānī. *Ḥilyat al-Awliyā' wa Ṭabaqāt al-Aṣfiyā'*. Beirut: Dār al-Fikr al-ʿArabī, 1974.

Bayhaqī, Abū Bakr Aḥmad ibn al-Ḥusayn. *Al-Asmā' wa'ṣ-Ṣifāt*. Jeddah: Maktabat as-Sawādī, 1993.

———. *Ad-Daʿawāt al-Kabīr*. Kuwait: Gharrās li'n-Nashr wa't-Tawzīʿ, 2009.

———. *Al-Qaḍā' wa'l-Qadr*. Riyadh: Maktabat Obeikan, 2000.

———. *Shuʿab al-Īmān*. Riyadh: Maktabah ar-Rushd al-Islāmiyyah, 2003.

———. *Az-Zuhd al-Kabīr*. Beirut: Mu'assasat al-Kutub ath-Thaqāfiyyah, 1996.

Bewley, A. and Bewley, A. A. *The Noble Qur'an: A New Rendering of its Meaning in English*. London: Ta-Ha Publishers, 2011.

Bukhārī, Muḥammad ibn Ismāʿīl. *Ṣaḥīḥ al-Bukhārī*. Beirut: Dār Ṭawq an-Najāt, 2002.

Dāraquṭnī, Abū 'l-Ḥasan ʿAlī ibn ʿUmar. *Sunan ad-Dāraquṭnī*. Beirut: Mu'assasat ar-Risālah, 2004.

Dhahabī, Shams ad-Dīn Muḥammad ibn Aḥmad. *Tārīkh al-Islām*. Beirut: Dār al-Gharb al-Islāmī, 2003.

Ḥākim, Muḥammad ibn ʿAbdullāh. *Al-Mustadrak ʿalā aṣ-Ṣaḥīḥayn*. Beirut: Dār al-Kutub al-ʿIlmiyyah, 1990.

Ibn Abī 'd-Dunyā, Abū Bakr ʿAbdullāh. *Awliyāʾ*. Beirut: Mu'assasat al-Kutub ath-Thaqāfiyyah, 1993.

———. *Al-Faraj baʿd ash-Shiddah*. Cairo: Dār ar-Rayyān, 1988.

———. (1993) *Mujābī ad-Daʿwah*. Beirut: Mu'assasat al-Kutub ath-Thaqāfiyyah.

———. *Ṣifat al-Jannah*. Cairo: Maktabat Ibn Taymiyyah, n.d.

Ibn Abī Ḥātim, Abū Muḥammad ʿAbd ar-Raḥmān ibn Muḥammad. *Tafsīr al-Qurʾān al-ʿAẓīm*. Riyadh: Maktabah Nazzār Muṣṭafā al-Bāz, 1998.

Ibn Bashkawāl, Abū 'l-Qāsim Khalaf ibn ʿAbd al-Malik. *Al-Mustaghīthīn bi'llāh*. Spain: al-Majlis al-Aʿlā li'l-Abḥāth al-ʿIlmiyyah Maʿhad at-Taʿāwun maʿ al-ʿĀlam al-ʿArabī, 1991.

Ibn Ḥibbān, Abū Ḥātim Muḥammad. *Ṣaḥīḥ Ibn Ḥibbān*. Beirut: Mu'assasat ar-Risālah, 1988.

Ibn al-Jawzī, Abū 'l-Faraj Jamāl ad-Dīn ʿAbd ar-Raḥmān. *Ṣayd al-Khāṭir*. Damascus: Dār al-Qalam, 2004.

Ibn Kathīr, Abū 'l-Fidā' Ismāʿīl ibn ʿUmar. *Tafsīr al-Qurʾān al-ʿAẓīm*. Riyadh: Dār Ṭaybah, 1999.

Ibn Mājah, Muḥammad ibn Yazīd al-Qazwīnī. *Sunan Ibn Mājah*. Cairo: Dār Iḥyā al-Kutub al-ʿArabiyyah, n.d.

Ibn Rajab, Zayn ad-Dīn ʿAbd ar-Raḥmān. (2008) *Nūr al-Iqtibās fī Mishkāt Waṣiyyat an-Nabī ṣalla Allāhu ʿalayhi wa sallam li-Ibn ʿAbbās*. Beirut: Dār al-Bashā'ir al-Islāmiyyah, 2008.

Ibn as-Sunnī, Aḥmad ibn Muḥammad ad-Dīnawarī. *ʿAmal al-Yawm wa'l-Laylah*. Jeddah: Dār al-Qiblah, n.d.

Mālik, ibn Anas al-Aṣbaḥī al-Madanī. *Muwaṭṭaʾ*. Abu Dhabi: Mu'assasat Zāyid bin Sulṭān, 2004.

Nasāʾī, Aḥmad ibn Shuʿayb. *As-Sunan al-Kubrā*. Beirut: Mu'assasat ar-Risālah, 2001.

———. *Sunan an-Nasāʾī*. Aleppo: Maktab al-Maṭbūʿāt al-Islāmiyyah, 1986.

Naysābūrī, Muslim ibn al-Ḥajjāj. *Ṣaḥīḥ Muslim*. Beirut: Dār Iḥyā' at-Turāth al-ʿArabī, n.d.

Ṣanʿānī, ʿAbd ar-Razzāq ibn Humām. *Muṣannaf*. Beirut: al-Maktab al-Islāmī, 1983.

Shāfiʿī, Muḥammad ibn Idrīs. *Musnad*. Beirut: Dār al-Kutub al-ʿIlmiyyah, 1980.

Shajarī, Yaḥyā ibn al-Ḥusayn al-Jurjānī. *Tartīb al-Amālī al-Khamsiyyah*. Beirut: Dār al-Kutub al-ʿIlmiyyah, 2001.

Shaybānī, Aḥmad ibn Ḥanbal. *Musnad al-Imām Aḥmad ibn Ḥanbal*. Beirut: Mu'assasat ar-Risālah, 2001.

Ṭabarānī, Abū 'l-Qāsim Sulaymān ibn Aḥmad. *Duʿā'*. Beirut: Dār al-Kutub al-ʿIlmiyyah, 1993.

———. *Al-Muʿjam al-Awsaṭ*. Cairo: Dār al-Ḥaramayn, n.d.

———. *Al-Muʿjam al-Kabīr*. Cairo: Maktabat Ibn Taymiyyah, 1994.

Ṭabarī, Abū Jaʿfar Muḥammad ibn Jarīr. *Jāmiʿ al-Bayān fī Ta'wīl al-Qur'ān*. Beirut: Mu'assasat ar-Risālah, 2000.

Tirmidhī, Abū ʿĪsā Muḥammad ibn ʿĪsā. *Al-Jāmiʿ al-Kabīr—Sunan at-Tirmidhī*. Beirut: Dār al-Gharb al-Islāmī, 1998.